cooking with a yogaview

a collection of recipes from the friends and family of yogaview

claire mark

Cooking with a yogaview: a collection of recipes from the friends and family of yogaview.
By Claire Mark

Edited by Jennifer Boeder
Photography by Scott Shigley
Back cover photo by Claire Mark
Design by Flockhart Design, Inc.

Printed in the United States of America
First Printing, 2012
ISBN-13: 978-0-615-65219-1

Printed by Palmer Printing, Inc.
Chicago, IL 60605

For more information, go to www.cookingwithayogaview.com.

THIS BOOK IS DEDICATED TO

my mom, for showing me how important good food is and how
wonderful it is to cook at home

Quinn Kearney and Tom Quinn, the founders of yogaview, for creating a safe and
beautiful space for people to practice yoga

and yogaview's teachers and students for continually showing up
I am so grateful to be a part of this amazing community

contents

Like yoga, cooking with real, organic foods grown and sold by people that you know increases your consciousness, connection, and nourishment. It helps to support a more open, conscious, and enlightened world.

Foreword
By Cassie Green

As the founder/owner of Green Grocer Chicago, the city's first local and organically focused small market, I've spent thousands of hours thinking about food, its sources, and the connection between us and what we eat. My own relationship with food has been as dramatic as a romance on a soap opera. I've had phases of eating no/low-carb and no/low-fat, eating fast food, inhaling nonsensical additives like Splenda, bingeing, drinking diet soda, counting calories, eschewing real butter for something called butter spray (don't ask)…the list goes on. During these phases, my energy level was in the toilet, and I certainly wasn't enjoying what I was eating.

Seven years ago, I read *This Organic Life* by Joan Gussow, which completely shifted my perspective on food and ultimately led me to create the Green Grocer. I wrote the author a very, very appreciative thank-you note! You see, I had never had a consciousness about how food was grown, where it was grown, who grew it, and what happened to me when I ate it.

I realized that food is one of the most basic connections we have to our planet, to our health, and to one another. With that realization came the desire to eat in a way that was positive for my body, kept chemicals out of our soil, air, and water, and brought people together over beautiful, delicious, and thoughtful meals. And because eating is the one thing we do three times a day that affects our health more than anything else, it seems like the wisest place for me to invest my resources.

Don't get me wrong: the time and money you have to spend in order to eat consciously is a real investment. But when you eat real food, grown in the ground, with a minimum of stress to the environment, or food that comes from animals that are treated humanely, you invest not only in your own health, but the health of our soil, our water sources, our local farming economies. And eating real foods (organic whenever possible) *can* be affordable. By spending a little time preparing food and purchasing wisely, you can easily save money at the register. For me, this means buying bulk dried beans and grains, making my own soup stocks, participating in local farm shares, eating in season as much as possible, having a little garden on our back deck, eating a very small amount of pasture-raised meat, and preparing large portions of meals in advance and eating them throughout the week.

And what's better in those moments than having a gorgeous cookbook to page through until that day's food inspiration hits you? That's why this book is so perfect. It's full of locally created recipes that will guide you towards eating more whole foods—and it's proof positive that you can eat more healthily without sacrificing taste or pleasure. Like yoga, cooking with real, organic foods grown and sold by people that you know increases your consciousness, connection, and nourishment. It helps to support a more open, conscious, and enlightened world. So make a cup of tea, find your favorite chair, turn the page, and get ready to cook!

Introduction

By Claire Mark

Much like good yoga, good food makes you feel full, warm, cozy, and complete--both have the potential to nourish and heal us on so many levels. For me, yoga and cooking are essential sources of energy, wellness, learning, and joy. As a yoga teacher and enthusiastic cook, I take great pleasure in sharing yoga and food with others, and I decided to create a cookbook that connected my love for both.

Yogaview, my home studio, celebrated its ten-year anniversary in July 2012, and putting this book together is my way of honoring this occasion, as well as yogaview's founders, Quinn Kearney and Tom Quinn, and the teachers and students who make up our extraordinary community. I began by asking yogaview teachers if they would donate a recipe to the cause; they responded with their characteristic enthusiasm and flooded my inbox with original and inventive dishes. Longtime students and friends of the studio joined in, including renowned chefs and restaurateurs whose contributions I am thrilled and honored to have. All of the contributors gave recipes freely in the spirit of sharing their favorite culinary creations with others, and the results are a virtual "potluck" of dishes that you can enjoy any time you open this book.

These recipes were chosen to appeal to a wide range of cooking skills and styles; they range from simple dishes with quick prep time for novice cooks, to more complex and sophisticated recipes for seasoned chefs. All of them feature healthy, whole foods, without additives, chemicals, or fake meats. We've included some fish dishes for pescatarians, as well as a host of vegetarian and vegan recipes.

Our goal was to create a cookbook with recipes full of flavor, spice, richness, and taste. We feel strongly that nutritious food need not be bland or boring, and we tested, fine-tuned, and savored all of the recipes offered here.

We also wanted to make it easier and more appealing for people to bring meat-free, local, and organic cuisine into their diets. We want to encourage everyone to stay conscious about where their food comes from, because our choices about food affect not only our health, but the health of our planet.

Lastly, we are donating 10% of all the proceeds from this book to the Cooking Up Change cooking contest, a fundraiser presented by the Healthy Schools Campaign with the goal of transforming public school food. Cooking Up Change educates public school children and their communities about how to create affordable, nourishing meals, and strives to change school food policy so that all children have access to nutritious, real food. For more information on this amazing organization and how to attend the Chicago event, see page 138.

In the same way that yogaview is comprised of the viewpoints and energies of many different and wonderful teachers and students, this book is a compilation of the culinary skills of a truly singular and vibrant yoga community, one I am blessed to be part of. I hope this book helps you breathe new life into your kitchen, and that you enjoy using it as much as we enjoyed creating it.

"

This book is a compilation of the culinary
skills of a truly singular and vibrant yoga
community, one I am blessed to be part of.

Yogaview's resident gourmet Vivian Roumboulas was our head food tester for this project.

Kitchen Tips from Vivian Roumboulas, Recipe Tester

Equipment

Theses items I personally couldn't do without:

Oven thermometer.
As a Chicago city dweller, I've moved at least three times in the last six years, and have had to cook on several stoves. Having a thermometer in my oven allows me to adjust the dial so that I don't ruin recipes (25 degrees makes a big difference). You can get one for as little as $7—no need to get fancy.

Good knives.
You don't need many. I use a chef's knife, a paring knife, and a serrated tomato/bread knife for almost everything. I like the weight of my Wusthof knife, but Global knives are considerably cheaper and lighter, and still excellent quality to get the job done.

A cast-iron skillet.
Lodge sells cast iron pre-seasoned these days so there's no reason why you shouldn't have a piece of inexpensive cast iron. There are several great reasons to use cast iron: it's an ideal heat conductor, it heats evenly and consistently, it's affordable, and a well-maintained cast-iron pan will last you a lifetime. When well seasoned, a cast-iron pan will be stick-resistant and require no additional oil. Even better, cooking with cast iron significantly boosts the iron content of your food.

Heavy bottomed stockpot/Dutch oven.
I like enameled cast iron, because it can easily go from stovetop to oven. I use this pot for almost all my soups and stews.

Food processor.
In testing the recipes for this book, I probably used my food processor more than I have since I purchased it. If you don't have a food processor, almost everything in these recipes can be done by hand, it just may take a little longer.

Stainless steel ½ sheet pans.
I use these to roast veggies or bake cookies.

Stand mixer.
If you're an avid baker, a stand mixer will produce great results and is worth the investment. It's not necessary, but will make cakes and cookies a breeze.

Guidelines for Using this Book

Whenever possible, use organic, locally grown and made products.

When using these recipes, always assume that:

– *All eggs are large.*
– *All butter is unsalted.*
– *Salt is always kosher (unless otherwise specified).*
– *Olive oil is always extra virgin.*
– *Flour is unbleached, all–purpose (unless otherwise specified).*

• When possible, use whole milk, cheese, and yogurt—less processing!
• When baking, eggs and butter should be room temperature.
• Measure dry ingredients in dry measuring cups.
• Measure wet ingredients in liquid measuring cups.
• If you're an avid baker, or interested in international cookbooks, invest in a scale (the results will change your life).
• When measuring flour, spoon it into measuring cups, then level off with a knife. **Don't** scoop with the measuring cup or pack it.

I suggest you read through your intended recipe at least twice before you begin, and have all your ingredients prepped and ready within reach before starting.

Happy cooking!

gratitude

Natarajasana—Lord of the Dance Pose
The Bean, Millennium Park

Practicing yoga and preparing meals offer us constant opportunities to be grateful, whether for our bodies or for the food on our plates. Gratitude enriches each experience and allows us to truly savor all that we have.

soups

Curried Sweet Potato Peanut Soup

Dorie Silverman, yogaview instructor

This soup is not only delicious, it's literally stove-to-table in under 30 minutes. In addition, sweet potatoes are a good source of vitamin D, which is both critical for our immune system function and harder to come by during the winter months. —Dorie

Preparation time: 25 minutes
Total time: 25 minutes
Serves 4

2 lbs. sweet potatoes, cut into small cubes
4-8 cups of vegetable stock

2 teaspoons curry powder
⅓ cup peanut butter or almond butter
salt to taste

Put cubed sweet potatoes in a large stock pot. Add enough stock to cover all of the potatoes. Bring to a boil and then simmer about 20 minutes or long enough to make the potatoes soft.

Turn off heat and stir in curry powder and about 1/3 cup of nut butter. Keep stirring until nut butter has melted into the soup. With a hand blender, puree the soup in the stock pot. Add salt to taste.

Spicy Vegetable Winter Soup

Claire Mark, yogaview instructor

I created this soup one afternoon on a cold winter day when I could feel a bad cold coming on. As a kid my mom always made chicken soup for us when we were sick, so I wanted something that replicated that idea but that was vegetarian. I added jalapeño to cleanse the sinuses, and some ginger and dark greens for their heating and healing properties. —Claire

Preparation time: 35-40 minutes
Total time: 45 minutes
Serves 4

2 tablespoons olive oil
4 large carrots, peeled and diced
2 celery stalks, minced
1 onion, minced
2 garlic cloves, minced
1 small piece fresh ginger, minced
1 small jalapeño, de-seeded and minced
1 32 oz. box veggie stock

1 cup water
1 cup white wine
1 bunch greens (kale, collard, or chard) cleaned, de-stemmed, and cut into bite-sized pieces
Optional: can of tomatoes or cut-up chunks of Yukon Gold potatoes, to add thickness

In a large pot on stove, heat olive oil, and then add garlic and sauté for several minutes, till garlic browns slightly. Add carrots, celery, onion, ginger, and jalapeño. Cook until onion is translucent, carrots are soft, and bottom of pot is starting to brown (about 15 to 20 minutes).

Add wine to de-glaze pot, then add veggie stock and water and bring to a boil. Add greens and (if adding) optional tomatoes/potatoes; cook for about 15 minutes, then salt and pepper to taste.

Serve while hot.

Chilled Cucumber Soup

Carole Mark, friend of yogaview

My mom came up with this recipe one summer, when the cucumbers in her garden did so well and she had so many that she had to find new ways to use them. —Claire

Preparation time: 15 minutes
Total time: 2½ to 6 hours
Serves 2

1½ cucumbers, pared and seeded
2 tablespoons olive oil
1 teaspoon salt (or less)
¼ teaspoon white pepper (or less)

1 clove garlic (or more) minced
2 teaspoons fresh dill, chopped
1 to 1½ cups yogurt

Mix oil, salt, pepper, garlic, and dill together. Marinate cucumber in this mixture for 2-6 hours in refrigerator, then puree mixture in blender. When ready to serve, add yogurt.

Easy Vegetable Stock

Vivian Roumboulas, yogaview student

You can buy boxed vegetable stock, but homemade really does taste better! —Vivian

Preparation time: 20 minutes
Total time: 2½ hours, makes approximately 3½ quarts

2 small onions, peeled and quartered
2-3 cloves garlic, peeled
½ an apple, peeled, cut into large chunks
2 carrots, scrubbed clean, cut into large chunks
2 stalks celery, cleaned, cut into large chunks (leaves optional)

1 large potato, scrubbed clean, quartered
1 tablespoon mixed peppercorns
2 bay leaves
sprigs of thyme
sprigs of parsley
1 tablespoon salt
1 gallon water

Put all ingredients in a large stockpot or in a slow cooker.

If using a slow cooker, set on low, and leave on overnight. If using stockpot, bring to a boil and cook at a simmer for 60 to 90 minutes.

When finished, strain stock through a cheesecloth or strainer and add salt to taste if needed. Use immediately or freeze in 16-32 oz. containers.

Roasted Carrot and Ginger Soup

Claire Mark, yogaview instructor

Adding the sweet potato to this soup makes it rich and smooth. One of ginger's biggest benefits is its ability to help sore muscles, so if you're doing a lot of yoga add some more ginger to this recipe! —Claire

Preparation time: 50 minutes
Total time: 50 minutes
Serves 4

1¼ lbs. carrots (about 10 total, depending on size) peeled and cut into French fry-sized sticks
4 cloves garlic
32 oz. (1 box) veggie stock
1 sweet potato, peeled and cut into small pieces

2 to 3 tablespoons grated fresh ginger
3 or more tablespoons olive oil
salt to taste

Preheat the oven to 425°. Put the carrots and garlic on a sheet pan, then drizzle with olive oil and salt and mix until evenly coated. Spread carrots evenly on sheet pan. Cook in the oven until carrots are starting to brown (20-25 minutes). Put stock into a pot over medium heat. When the carrots and garlic are browned, add them to the pot with the grated ginger and sweet potato. Cook for 20 minutes on medium/high heat until sweet potatoes are soft. Use a hand blender to puree soup in the pot.

Optional: garnish with a dollop of yogurt and some minced parsley or chives.

Miso Vegetable Soup

Jessica Quinn, wife of Tom Quinn, co-founder of yogaview

Our family is Irish, and there are many old seaweed soup recipes from Ireland. In this one I added my own touch. —Jessica

Preparation time: 25 minutes
Total time: 25 minutes
Serves 4

8 cups of vegetable broth
2½ tablespoons fresh miso
½ cup of carrots, cut and coined into halves
1 cup shiitake or cremini mushrooms
1 cup of broccoli, chopped into half-inch pieces

2 cups udon noodles
2 cups dried or fresh kelp seaweed, cut on an angle into small pieces (it will expand when added to the soup)
4 eggs, hard boiled
4 tablespoons of chives or green onions (for garnish)

Pour all the broth into a pot and scoop in the miso. Simmer (do not boil) the broth and stir the miso to break it up in the broth.

Add carrots and broccoli, cook for about 10 minutes.

Add seaweed, mushrooms, and noodles, cook for another 10 minutes (or until the noodles are tender).

Pour into a bowl and serve as is, or top with a sliced hard-boiled egg. Garnish with fresh chives or green onions (a tablespoon for each bowl).

Cold Curried Tomato Soup

Audrey Fosse, yogaview student

This is an ideal soup to make on a hot summer day when you don't want to turn on the stove. —Vivian

Preparation time: 20 minutes
Total time: 20 minutes
Serves 4

1 cup plain yogurt (8 oz)
3 cups tomato juice
1 tablespoon olive oil
1 tablespoon fresh lemon juice
 (or more to taste)
1 tablespoon red wine vinegar

4 drops Tabasco (or to taste)
1½ teaspoons curry powder (or to taste)
1 shallot (½ oz.), finely chopped
dash of salt and white pepper
parsley, chopped for garnish

Stir the yogurt with a wire whisk until smooth.

Mix in the remaining ingredients, except parsley.

Adjust quantities to taste.

Serve in mugs with fresh parsley sprinkled on top.

Parsnip and Fingerling Potato Soup

Vivian Roumboulas, yogaview student

This is a great winter soup for cold nights—hearty and comforting. —Vivian

Preparation time: 30 minutes
Total time: 30 minutes
Serves 6 (as an entrée)

1-2 tablespoons olive oil
10 medium-sized parsnips, peeled and cut
   into 2-inch pieces
½ lb. fingerling potatoes of your choice
5-6 extra potatoes, cut into thin slices
2 quarts vegetable stock

½ teaspoon nutmeg
½ cup half and half or cream
crème fraîche or sour cream and parsley
   for serving
salt and freshly ground pepper

Preheat oven to 425°. Heat stock in large stockpot.

Take the ½ lb. of fingerling potatoes, cut them in half, and then combine them with the parsnips. Salt, pepper, and toss them with olive oil.

In single layer lay out seasoned potatoes and parsnips on a sheet pan. Roast until browning around the edges and fragrant (about 20-25 minutes).

Remove roasted veggies, take reserved 5-6 fingerling potatoes and slice them paper thin. Salt and pepper them and place on a roasting pan in a single layer (you can re-use sheet pan from parsnips). Place in oven and cook until crispy and brown. Remove and set aside for garnish later.

Once stock is boiling, add roasted parsnips/potatoes to stock pot, and cook until tender (about 15 but up to 35 minutes) over medium heat.

Turn off heat. Allow to cool for about 5-10 minutes, then slowly drizzle in cream, being careful not to dump it all in at once.

Add nutmeg, then taste and adjust salt and pepper as necessary.

To serve, ladle into bowls, add a spoonful of crème fraîche in the center, top with remaining potato slices and parsley.

Soup of Sunshine

Richards Career Academy culinary students

The Cooking Up Change healthy cooking contest challenges Chicago Public School culinary students to create recipes for a healthy school lunch (think "Top Chef" for teenagers). They work within a tight budget, and with limited ingredients and specific nutrition standards, so the team from Richards Career Academy knew they would have to think outside the box. Following a Caribbean cuisine theme, the students designed a meal with bright flavors and innovative ingredient combinations that wowed guests and judges alike.

Many thanks to student chefs Gerardo Garcia, Ruby Gutierrez, Claudia Ramirez, and Lidia Sanchez for sharing this wonderful recipe! Check out healthyschoolscampaign.org for more great recipes from these amazing young chefs, and to learn more about Cooking Up Change and their mission of changing school food for the better.

Preparation time: 30 minutes
Total time: 40 minutes
Serves 4

1 medium Spanish onion
1 large green bell pepper
2 small apples
1½ bananas
1 tablespoon vegetable or grapeseed oil
6 cups vegetable stock (see page 13 for recipe if you'd like to make your own)
1 15 oz. can diced tomatoes with juice

1 cup frozen yellow squash, sliced
¼ cup peanut butter
⅛ teaspoon garlic powder
⅛ teaspoon chili powder
⅛ teaspoon paprika
¼ teaspoon black pepper
3 tablespoons coarsely chopped cilantro

Dice onion, bell peppers, apples, and banana into ½ inch pieces. Heat oil in large pot. Add onions, bell pepper, and apples; gently sauté until softened. Add stock and bring to a boil.

Add bananas, squash, diced tomatoes, peanut butter, cilantro and all spices; continue to boil for one minute, and then reduce to a simmer.

Gently simmer for 15-20 minutes or until produce is tender; add cilantro. Taste and adjust seasoning to desired flavor.

Parsnip Soup

Tamiz Haiderali, Township Restaurant

Parsnip is an underrated root vegetable. It is one of the best offerings of the fall season. This recipe is quick, easy, and the results are unexpectedly delicious. It can be prepared vegan and light, or with butter and cream for extra richness. —*Tamiz*

Preparation time: 30 minutes
Total time: 30 minutes
Serves 6

5 medium-sized (or 3 cups) parsnips, peeled and cubed
1 peeled parsnip (for garnish)
1 medium onion, diced
½ cup celery stalks or fennel stalks, diced
½ cup carrots, peeled and diced
1 tablespoon chopped garlic
4 cups vegetable broth

½ cup heavy cream (optional)
1½ tablespoons butter (optional)
1½ tablespoons olive oil (use 3 tablespoons olive oil if making vegan/ not including butter and/or cream)
1 teaspoon ground white pepper
2 bay leaves
salt to taste

Heat oil (and butter, if using) in a pan. When hot, add onions and cook till translucent, stirring often. Add garlic, carrots, and celery and continue to stir. When vegetables are soft and the mixture is cooked, add bay leaf and black pepper and stir for 30 seconds. Add parsnips (minus one set aside for garnish) stock, and cream (if using) and bring to a boil. Simmer till parsnips are fully cooked through (they should be soft and fall apart when poked with a fork). Let cool, remove bay leaves, and puree mixture in a blender (you may need to do this in batches). Check for salt and add to taste. Add more stock or return to heat and reduce for desired consistency.

Meanwhile, using a potato peeler, make thin long ribbons peeling the entire length of the parsnip (but do not peel core). In a deep fryer or wok, heat hot oil until very hot and then fry the parsnip ribbons for 1 minute. Make sure they are separate and not clumped together. Drain on a paper towel.

Pour parsnip soup in a bowl and top with ribbons. If parsnip ribbons are too time-consuming, dot the soup with an infused (herb or saffron) oil or just plain olive oil for dramatic plating.

Township is both a music venue and a restaurant in Logan Square; founded by the chef of Humboldt Park's beloved Treat restaurant, Township's menu offers hearty, healthy meals, often with a distinctly Indian bent. In addition to an amazing brunch, Township's extended evening hours provide a healthy alternative to typical late night meals.

Lentil and Chestnut Soup

Carolyn Rosenberg, yogaview student

This soup is simple, elegant, and super easy. The texture of the chestnuts makes this feel decadent even though it's not. I've made it several times since the initial testing, always to rave reviews. You can use any lentils, but it is worth it to find Puy (aka French) lentils as they make a heartier soup. This is now my go-to winter soup. —Vivian

Preparation time: 35-45 minutes
Total time: 45 minutes
Serves 4-6

1 ½ to 2 cups Puy (French) lentils (rinse them and check for small pebbles)
1 can or jar chestnuts (approx. 225 g), chopped (do not use fresh)
2 quarts of vegetable stock
2 sticks celery chopped (chopped leaves included)

2 carrots
1 medium onion
½ a leek (optional)
2 tablespoons butter or olive oil

For the garnish:
chopped parsley, sour cream, or crème fraîche

Finely chop onion, leek, carrot, and celery. Add to oil or butter in soup pan and sauté until soft. Add lentils and stock (1 quart to start). Bring to boil and simmer until lentils are soft (Puy lentils take about an hour and will probably need more stock; red lentils need the least amount of time and stock).

Add chestnuts and cook 20 minutes more (add water or more stock if too thick). Crush large chestnut bits and blend them into the soup—depending on how smooth you like your soup, you can blend completely or leave chunky. Garnish with parsley, crème fraîche, or sour cream.

Spicy Thai Coconut Soup

Valerie Bolon, yogaview student

Making Asian food can be intimidating for me—this soup, however, lets you create those authentic flavors in your own kitchen. It's as good as any I've had in a Thai restaurant.
—Claire

Preparation time: 30 minutes
Total time: 30 minutes
Serves 4 (as an entrée)

1-2 tablespoons red curry paste (depending on how spicy you prefer)
2 stalks lemongrass, rough cut into a few large pieces
2 roma tomatoes, rough chopped
½ white onion, rough chopped
4 cloves garlic, rough chopped
1 teaspoon fresh ginger, peeled and chopped
1-2 kaffir lime leaves (if available)

1 cup sliced shiitake mushrooms (or any mushrooms you prefer)
¼ cup cilantro, leaves picked and kept whole
2 cans coconut milk
4 cups vegetable stock or water
¼ cup fish sauce
1 tablespoon lime juice
1-2 tablespoons cooking oil (vegetable, safflower, or any light-colored oil can be used)

Place a large stockpot over medium heat. Add oil; once it's hot, add the onion and sauté until the onion becomes translucent (about 2-3 minutes). Add tomatoes, garlic, lemongrass, ginger, and lime leaves and sauté 2-3 more minutes. Add the curry paste and stir thoroughly. Let the mixture cook for about 3 minutes to release the flavor.

Then add fish sauce, lime juice, and stock and bring to a boil. Reduce the heat to medium and add the coconut milk. Let the soup simmer to infuse all the flavors for about 20 minutes. Taste the soup to make sure it has the desired spiciness.

To create more heat, simply add small amounts of curry paste slowly (it can get very spicy very quickly!) Be sure to taste frequently. Once desired flavor is achieved, remove the lemongrass and lime leaves.

To serve, add the mushrooms and heat for about 3 minutes. Add cilantro leaves to garnish.

Lula Café's casual, chic, and artistic atmosphere has made it a well-loved neighborhood fixture. Lula's fans extend far beyond Logan Square, however—co-owners and chefs Jason Hammel and Amalea Tshilds have received national recognition as leaders in the Chicago school of New American cuisine. They emphasize organic and artisanal ingredients in their dishes, create their menus based on availability from local farmers and markets, and deliver ever-changing but always delectable dishes.

Celery and Asian Pear Soup with Black Walnut Pesto

Jason Hammel and Lea Tshilds, Lula Café

In the summertime you can buy celery at most farmer's markets; this type of celery has many leaves and is often stronger in flavor. If you are looking for celery leaves and cannot find them on stalks of celery from the store, you may want to replace the leaves with the herb lovage, which, though not always easy to find, has a strong celery flavor. Your best bet is to look for full heads of celery, as opposed to chopped or hearts of celery.
—Lea

Preparation time: 60 minutes
Total time: 60 minutes
Serves 6

For the soup:
1 Vidalia onion, chopped
¼ head of fennel, chopped
1 head of celery, chopped and divided into two portions
⅛ cup dry vermouth
⅛ cup golden raisins
1 small Asian pear or ½ a large one, skin on
1 small yellow tomato
bouquet garni (parsley, bay, marjoram, thyme, black pepper, coriander, clove, fennel seed, and Parmesan rind in a cheesecloth bag)
2 quarts vegetable stock
1½ large Yukon gold potatoes, peeled and sliced
½ quart cream
½ (or more) tablespoon olive oil

For the pesto:
½ cup celery leaf
½ cup parsley leaf
⅛ cup toasted black walnuts
zest of half a lemon
2 cloves garlic
¼ cup Parmesan
1 tablespoon olive oil

In a stock pot, sweat the onion, fennel, and half of the celery in olive oil over low heat. De-glaze the pot with the vermouth by bringing to a boil and scraping the bottom of the pan with a wooden spoon. Add raisins, pear, and tomato, and cook until slightly softened.

Add bouquet garni, vegetable stock, potatoes, and remaining portion of celery to the pot. Cook until absolutely tender. Add the cream in small amounts, stirring after each addition to prevent curdling. Simmer briefly.

Remove bouquet garni and puree the soup gently (too much agitation can cause the cream to break).

While the soup is cooking, make the pesto. Put the celery leaves, parsley, walnuts, lemon zest, garlic, and Parmesan in the bowl of a food processor. Pulse until finely chopped. With the blade running, slowly drizzle in the olive oil until a pesto is formed. Serve the soup warm and top with the pesto.

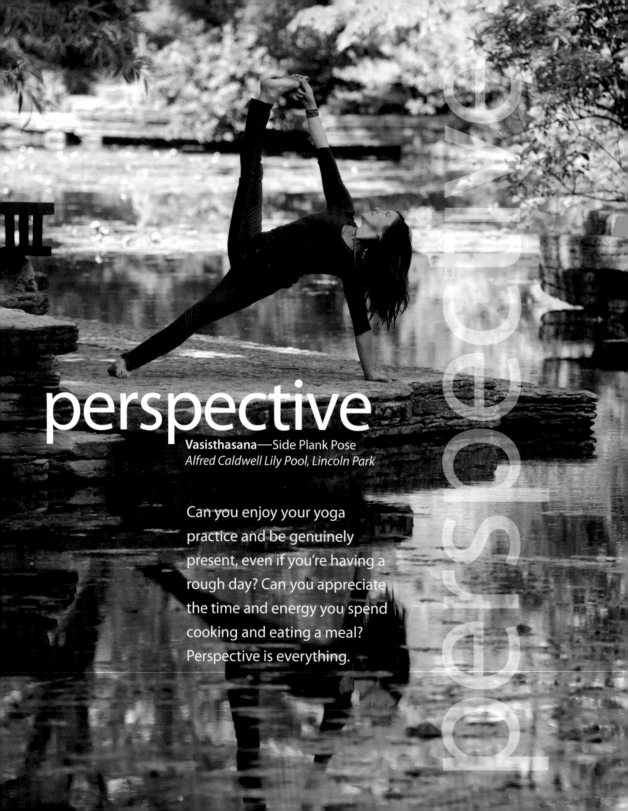

perspective

Vasisthasana—Side Plank Pose
Alfred Caldwell Lily Pool, Lincoln Park

Can you enjoy your yoga practice and be genuinely present, even if you're having a rough day? Can you appreciate the time and energy you spend cooking and eating a meal? Perspective is everything.

salads

Caprese Salad

Claire Mark, yogaview instructor

I love a classic caprese salad, but in the winter it's hard to find flavorful big tomatoes--this recipe is great because you can find cherry tomatoes all year round. The olives add extra salty flavor and are full of heart-healthy fats, which can help to lower cholesterol. —Claire

Preparation time: 10 minutes
Total time: 10 minutes
Serves 2-4

1 pint of small fresh mozzarella balls, each cut in half
1 pint of cherry tomatoes, each cut in half
1 bunch of fresh basil, shredded

8 pitted calamata olives, each cut in half
½ cup olive oil
¼ cup balsamic vinegar
salt and black pepper (to taste)

Whisk olive oil and balsamic together for dressing. Mix other ingredients together in a bowl, toss with dressing, add salt and pepper to taste, and serve.

Arugula and Fennel Salad

Claire Mark, yogaview instructor

The fennel in this salad not only adds amazing flavor and aroma, but is high in vitamin C and excellent for digestion. —Claire

Preparation time: 10 minutes
Total time: 10 minutes
Serves 2-4

8 oz. bag of arugula or 1-2 heads arugula (depending on size of heads)
1 fennel bulb, very thinly sliced (use a mandolin slicer if available)
½ cup Parmesan cheese strips, sliced thin with a vegetable peeler

For the dressing:
½ cup olive oil
¼ cup fresh lemon juice
sea salt

Whisk olive oil and lemon juice and add salt to taste. Toss gently with other ingredients and serve.

Caesar Salad

Quinn Kearney, yogaview co-founder

This is a great recipe I learned years ago when I was living in Toronto. The homemade croutons add a little warmth to the salad. —Quinn

Preparation time: 20 minutes
Total time: 20 minutes
Serves 2-4

For the croutons:
2 pieces of bread (sourdough or wheat work best) cut into ¼-inch pieces
enough olive oil to coat the bottom of a frying pan

Heat a frying pan, and once it's hot, add the oil to the pan. When the oil is warm, add the cut-up bread pieces and mix it around in the pan immediately so that the bread is evenly coated with the olive oil. Occasionally mix the bread around in the pan until it is toasted, crispy, and brown. Remove the pan from the heat and let it cool.

For the salad:
1 large head of romaine lettuce

Wash lettuce and tear into bite-sized pieces.

For the dressing:
2 cloves garlic
juice from ½ lemon
3 dashes Worcestershire sauce
30 grinds of pepper (just under
    ½ tablespoon)
1 tablespoon Dijon mustard

½ teaspoon of salt
2-3 anchovies (optional)
2 tablespoons Parmesan cheese
½ cup olive oil
a tiny bit of water to blend

In a food processor or blender, blend all ingredients except the olive oil and Parmesan cheese at low speed; as you blend, gradually add in olive oil, and then the Parmesan. Taste and check oil/lemon balance, and then dress salad and add croutons and more Parmesan cheese to taste.

Emerald Kale Salad

Carolyn Rosenberg, yogaview student

Preparation time: 15 minutes
Total time: 15 minutes
Serves 2-4

I'm not normally a fan of raw kale, but testing this salad converted me--I made it for many days in a row after my initial test! The lemon juice and hand-mixing slightly "cooks" and softens the raw kale to an emerald green. This is an easy way to get more raw greens in your diet. —Jennifer

1 large bunch kale
¼ cup grated Parmesan (or more to taste)
¼ pine nuts
juice from 1 lemon
zest from same lemon
2 tablespoons olive oil
1 teaspoon salt (or more to taste)

Wash and chop kale, removing thick stems. Blend pine nuts and Parmesan in a small food processor (you can also grind them together in a nut grinder or coffee grinder, or simply chop or crush them till powdery).

Add lemon juice and salt to kale to taste, then mix with your hands, squeezing kale until slightly wilted and bright green.

Add olive oil, Parmesan/pine nut mixture, and lemon zest. Toss and serve.

Pine Nut and Quinoa Salad

Carole Mark, friend of yogaview

Cultivated in the Andes for over 5,000 years, quinoa has been called the "mother grain" and "the gold of the Incas." Today, the popularity of quinoa (pronounced KEEN-wah) is growing steadily as people discover its pleasant nutty taste and superfood qualities. It's not only a complete protein source, but also high in iron, magnesium, and fiber.

If you'd like to make this dish vegan, just substitute vegetable oil for the butter (I use Earth Balance). —Carole

Preparation time: 20 minutes
Total time: 50 minutes (including time to soak the currants)
Serves 4

3 cups vegetable stock
1½ cups quinoa (see quinoa instructions for ratio of quinoa to water, as different brands may vary)
2 tablespoons butter
1 teaspoon saffron
1½ cups diced celery
⅔ cup currants, soaked in hot water for 15 minutes

⅓ cup scallions, thinly sliced
⅓ cup pine nuts, lightly toasted
½ cup parsley leaves, minced

For the dressing:
¼ cup lemon juice
¼ teaspoon cinnamon
½ cup olive oil

Rinse quinoa thoroughly. Simmer stock in a pot. Bring it to a boil, add saffron and butter, then add quinoa and cover and let simmer till water absorbed (15-20 minutes).

In a large bowl, combine celery, currants, pine nuts, scallions, and parsley and toss.

Whisk lemon and cinnamon into olive oil, then add to the tossed vegetables.

Add slightly cooled quinoa to mixture. Mix well and serve.

Amethyst Asian Slaw

Dorie Silverman, yogaview instructor

Dorie threw this salad together one evening for a backyard barbecue, and it was so amazing I immediately asked if we could have her recipe for the cookbook. Umeboshi vinegar is a bright red seasoning made from pickled Japanese plums; that, plus the purple cabbage, give this dish a gorgeous color. Added bonus: cabbage is rich in vitamin C, vitamin K, and antioxidants. —Jennifer

Preparation time: 10 minutes
Total time: 10 minutes
Serves 4 (as a side dish)

One half head purple cabbage, sliced thin
¼ cup sesame oil (regular, not toasted)
⅛ cup umeboshi vinegar

1 inch of ginger, finely grated
black sesame seeds

Mix all the above ingredients in a bowl, saving the sesame seeds for last so they will stick better to the cabbage. Serve immediately for maximum crunchiness.

Cucumber Salad

Nicole Thompson, yogaview instructor

Cucumbers are a great source of fiber, potassium, antioxidants, and Vitamin K. —Claire

Preparation time: 10 minutes
Total time: 40 minutes
Serves 4

2 medium-sized cucumbers, peeled and sliced thinly

For the dressing:
1 tablespoon soy sauce
2 tablespoon toasted sesame oil

1 tablespoon sugar
1 tablespoon white rice vinegar
½ tablespoon salt
1¼ tablespoon Tabasco
  (do not omit—it's the key to the salad)

Mix all ingredients until sugar is well dissolved. Pour over cucumbers, making sure to coat all slices. Chill for 30 minutes to allow flavor to absorb into cucumbers and serve.

Mango Avocado Salad

Tiffin Kearney Bolger, friend of yogaview

This salad has great color, texture, sweetness , and spice, as well as an ideal balance of proteins, healthy fats, and fruit. —Tiffin

Preparation time: 20 minutes
Total time: 20 minutes
Serves 4-6

2 mangoes, diced
1 jalapeño, no seeds, diced
1 can black beans, rinsed and drained
⅛ cup diced red onion
¼ cup cilantro
3 avocados, diced
½ lemon, squeezed
¼ teaspoon salt

For the dressing:
2 tablespoons olive oil
1 tablespoon lemon juice
1 tablespoon cider vinegar
¼ teaspoon cumin
¼ teaspoon salt
¼ teaspoon cayenne pepper

Mix dressing. Combine with mango, jalapeño, beans, onion, and cilantro. Right before serving, mix avocados with lemon juice and salt and carefully fold into salad.

Simple Salad with Citrus Dressing

Amy Schatz, yogaview instructor

The tart/sweetness of this dressing is outstanding—you can use it over almost any variation of greens. —Vivian

Preparation time: 15 minutes
Total time: 15 minutes
Serves 2-4

For the dressing:

3 tablespoons orange juice
1 tablespoon lime juice
1 tablespoon grapefruit juice
1 tablespoon lemon juice
1 tablespoon white wine vinegar

½ cup olive oil
3 tablespoons Dijon mustard
2-3 tablespoons honey
1 clove garlic, crushed
1 tablespoon shallot, chopped

Mix above ingredients and set aside.

For the salad:

1–2 heads of butter lettuce or Boston
   red leaf lettuce, washed and chopped
⅔ cup sliced almonds

3 oz. feta cheese, crumbled
   (I prefer to use a brick, then crumble)
salt and pepper to taste

Combine lettuce, almonds, and feta in a bowl. Add dressing, plus salt and pepper to taste, and serve.

Grilled Radicchio Salad with Arugula, Black Olives, and Feta

Claire Mark, yogaview instructor

This salad tastes fresh and crisp; grilling the radicchio makes it much less bitter and brings out its natural nutty flavor. —Claire

Preparation time: 20 minutes
Total time: 20 minutes
Serves 2-4

For the dressing:
3 tablespoons olive oil
1½ tablespoons balsamic vinegar
1 garlic clove, minced

1 teaspoon Dijon mustard
1 teaspoon lemon juice
1 pinch of salt

For the salad:
1 head radicchio
8 oz. (1 bag or one head) arugula

¼ cup of feta cheese, crumbled
   (more if you're a cheese lover!)
5 pitted black olives, cut in half

Place a grill pan on the stove over high heat. Cut the head of radicchio into quarters and brush them with olive oil. Place them on the grill pan, turning them every few minutes until they are brown, then remove them from the heat and cut into bite-sized pieces.

In a large salad bowl, place the arugula, radicchio, and black olives. Combine all the ingredients for the dressing in a small jar and shake them well.

Pour the dressing on the greens and mix well. Add the crumbled feta and serve.

Arugula and Beet Salad with Pistachios

Amy Schatz, yogaview instructor

Balsamic glaze is a reduction you can make by putting balsamic vinegar in a small saucepan over low heat, and cooking it until it "reduces" (i.e., much of the liquid evaporates) by half; a glaze will be more syrupy and sweeter than the vinegar. —Amy

Preparation time: 15 minutes
Total time: 75 minutes
Serves 4

6 to 8 small beets (mix red and yellow beets for the tricolor effect)
1 8 oz. bag arugula
⅔ cup pistachios, toasted and chopped small
½ cup goat cheese
freshly ground pepper

1½ - 2 tablespoons balsamic glaze (or, if you don't want to make the glaze, just balsamic vinegar)
5 tablespoons olive oil (2 reserved to dress salad after beets are cooked)
sea salt

Preheat oven to 350°.

Cover a baking sheet with a sheet of aluminum foil, and lay the beets on it. Lightly drizzle beets with olive oil and salt. Cover the beets with aluminum foil and seal the edges. Bake for 1 hour or until the beets are tender.

Peel the beets and cut them into quarter slices.

Arrange arugula on a platter. Put the beets and pistachio pieces on top. Crumble the goat cheese over the salad. Add the olive oil, salt, and pepper to taste. Lightly drizzle with the balsamic glaze or vinegar.

Located in Chicago's West Loop, the Publican is a beer-focused restaurant that evokes an old-world European beer hall. Executive Chef Paul Kahan and Chef de Cuisine Brian Huston crafted Publican's eclectic menu inspired by simple farmhouse fare.

Grilled Asparagus with Caesar Dressing

Brian Huston, the Publican

This recipe is something we've been doing this spring at the Publican. It's a great Caesar recipe—this dressing can be used in hearty salads as well as on grilled or steamed vegetables. —Brian

1-1½ pounds standard or jumbo
    asparagus
2 tablespoons olive oil
salt

Caesar dressing:

1 tablespoon red wine vinegar
⅔ cup olive oil
1 tablespoon chopped anchovies
2 teaspoons chopped garlic

2 eggs
3 oz. Parmesan cheese
juice of one lemon
½ teaspoon black pepper

Prepare the grill by lighting the coals and letting them burn until they reach an even glow. Spread the coals and preheat the grill for a minute.

For the asparagus:
Break off the woody ends of the asparagus and peel away the skin from an inch from the tip. Bring a large pot of water to a boil. Salt water lightly, about a tablespoon of salt per gallon of water. Blanch the asparagus for about one minute. Drain and cool in ice water for about three minutes or until cooled through. Drain and pat dry with a towel. Oil the asparagus and arrange in a single layer on the grill. Grill until hot, about 2 minutes per side.

For the dressing:
In a bowl, whisk together the vinegar, oil, anchovies, and garlic. Add the eggs and grate about 1/3 of the Parmesan into the bowl. Continue to whisk and add the lemon juice and black pepper. The dressing should emulsify.

On a serving platter, lay out the asparagus and drizzle dressing over the asparagus. For garnish, using a peeler, peel the rest of the Parmesan into shards all over the dish.

Sweet Potato Salad

Sara Strother, yogaview instructor

Although traditional potato salad has never been my favorite, sometimes it's the only vegetarian option at the neighborhood barbeque. So I developed a potato salad alternative that is chock-full of good stuff.

When making this salad, be sure to serve immediately while the avocado dressing still retains its green color. —Sara

Preparation time: 20 minutes
Total time: 30 minutes
Serves 4-6

2 sweet potatoes, chopped into
  1-inch pieces
1 large fennel bulb, diced

1 celery stalk, diced
1 cup chopped red onion

Fill a pot with 2 ounces of water over high heat and place a steaming basket on top. Chop the sweet potato into cubes; once the water boils, steam potatoes until tender. Remove from the basket and let cool.

For the dressing:

2 avocados, cubed
1 large handful of fresh basil leaves
2 teaspoons olive oil

2 teaspoons fresh lemon or lime juice
1 garlic clove, peeled and minced
sea salt and black pepper, to taste

Combine basil, garlic, and a pinch of sea salt in a small food processor and blend until ingredients form a paste. Add avocados and process until smooth. Blend in the oil and lemon or lime juice, and then season with sea salt and pepper.

In a large bowl, place fennel, onion, celery, and cooled sweet potato. Pour over the avocado mayo and turn gently with a wooden spoon to dress.

Watercress and Arugula Salad with Pear and Sunchokes

Vivian Roumboulas, yogaview student

A sunchoke, also known as a Jerusalem artichoke, has crisp white flesh and a texture similar to jicama or a water chestnut. They contain more than three times the iron as an equal serving of broccoli, plus vitamins B and C. —Vivian

Preparation time: 20 minutes
Total time: 45 minutes
Serves 4 generously or 6 as an accompaniment to a meal

1 bunch or 8 oz. bag arugula, washed carefully

1 bunch watercress

2 small sunchokes, peeled and julienned or cut into thin discs (hold in water with lemon to keep from browning if doing this part ahead of time)

1 ripe but firm green pear of your choice, sliced thin

2 oz. chevre or crumbled goat cheese of your choosing (omit to make vegan)

½-¾ cup Candied Chipotle Walnuts (see recipe page 135)

For the dressing:

⅓ cup champagne or sherry vinegar

⅔ cup mild olive oil

2 tablespoons minced shallot

1 tablespoon honey

salt and pepper to taste

Combine dressing ingredients and allow to sit at room temperature for at least ½ hour. Chop watercress and combine with arugula in non-reactive salad bowl.

Add sunchoke pieces and pear. Add walnuts, goat cheese crumbles, and dressing just before serving.

Sweet and Savory Spinach Salad

Erica Merrill, yogaview instructor

The extra minutes you take to grill the onions and corn for this salad are so worth it. Feel free to substitute any cheese of your choosing, or replace with avocado to make vegan. —Erica

Preparation time: 25 minutes
Total time: 30 minutes
Serves 4

10-12 oz. fresh spinach
2 ears sweet corn
½ red onion, chopped
1 orange pepper

⅓ cup pecans
⅓ cup dried cherries
1 tablespoon vegetable oil
crumbled gorgonzola

For the dressing:
¼ cup balsamic vinegar
¼ cup olive oil
1 tablespoon Dijon mustard

½ teaspoon lemon juice
pinch of ground sea salt
pepper to taste

Place spinach in large mixing bowl. Place skillet on high heat for two minutes.

Add vegetable oil, then add sliced corn and onion. Sauté until onion and corn brown slightly. Add to spinach and toss with the rest of vegetables and dressing. Top with gorgonzola.

Shaved Asparagus Salad with Parmesan and Mushroom Chips

Tara Mark, friend of yogaview

This recipe will turn out best when asparagus is in season (spring through early summer). Asparagus is full of antioxidants and is a great source of fiber, vitamin A, C, E, and K.
—Tara

Preparation time: 30 minutes
Total time: 30 minutes
Serves 4

1 bunch asparagus
2 oz. Parmesan cheese
4 mushrooms (trumpet, oyster, or any mushrooms you like) sliced very thin

juice of 1 lemon
⅓ cup olive oil, plus ¼ cup for mushrooms
salt to taste

Preheat oven to 350°. After slicing the mushrooms very thin, lay them out on a baking sheet and lightly brush with olive oil (not too much, as you want them crisp). Bake in the oven until crispy (about 15 minutes).

While they bake, take a vegetable peeler and shave the raw asparagus through the entire stalk (this part is time-consuming but worth it!). Put the shaved asparagus in a bowl and squeeze lemon juice on top; stir and set aside. Shave the Parmesan cheese with peeler and set aside.

When the mushrooms are done, remove from the oven and let them cool. Pour olive oil and salt over the asparagus and mix. Add cheese and mushroom chips on top, and you're ready to serve!

Shaved Brussels Sprout Salad with Brown Butter Vinaigrette

Koren Grieveson, Avec Restaurant

Shaving the Brussels sprouts is time-consuming, but the finished result is texturally so surprising and pretty that you may convert Brussels sprouts haters forever with this one!
—Vivian

Preparation time: 30 minutes
Total time: 30 minutes
Serves 4

For the dressing:

2 tablespoons butter, melted until just past golden
1 shallot, minced
3 cups orange juice, reduced to a syrupy consistency

¼ cup champagne vinegar
1 tablespoon olive oil
salt and pepper to taste

Whisk all the above ingredients together and season to taste. There should be enough acid to cut through the fat and enough saltiness to bring out the sweetness of the orange juice.

4 cups thinly sliced Brussels sprouts (using either a mandolin, or by hand)
2 cups very thinly shaved fennel (leave in cold water if cutting ahead of time)
½ red onion, very thinly sliced or shaved

¾ to 1 cup of shaved Parmesan or other good sweet and salty hard cheese
¼ cup roughly chopped dill and chives, together
lemon juice, salt, and pepper to taste

Place the Brussels sprouts, fennel, onion, Parmesan, and dill/chive mix into a large bowl. Toss with the dressing (you may not need all of it, do not overdress) and add lemon juice, salt, and pepper to taste. Toss well and serve.

Avec means "with" in French, which is an apt description, because Avec's diners drink wine with their food at communal tables with friends and neighbors, and many of the dishes are for sharing. Avec is first and foremost a wine bar, and its menu is decidedly Mediterranean, inspired by the wine-growing regions of Southern France, Italy, Portugal, and the Spanish coast. Chef de Cuisine Koren Grieveson was the recipient of the 2011 James Beard Foundation Award for Best Chef: Great Lakes/Midwest.

balance

Mayurasana—Peacock Pose
Fullerton Street Beach

Balance is essential to both our yoga practice and our food choices, whether it's making sure to eat a wide variety of fruits and vegetables, or surfing the edges of your foot in tree pose.

appetizers & sides

Pickles

Carole Mark, friend of yogaview

*To make pickles, you need a large jar (gallon or more) with a cap that can be
closed tightly. —Carole*

Preparation time: 10 minutes
Total time: minimum 1 day

½ gallon filtered water
3-4 tablespoons pickling salt
1 medium onion, quartered
4-6 cloves garlic
2 tablespoons coriander seeds
several sprigs of fresh dill

1-2 bay leaves
several dried hot peppers
  (more if you like your pickles hot)
8-10 unwaxed cucumbers, whole or
  sliced

Add salt to water. Add all other ingredients, alternating with cucumbers.

Let jar stand unrefrigerated for at least 12 hours (keep in mind the warmer the weather, the
shorter time to pickle before you refrigerate). In cooler weather, leave the jar out several days
for the vegetables to brine, then refrigerate jar.

Other vegetables one can pickle are endless! Experiment with your favorites.
Here are some I have used:

green tomatoes, quartered
blanched green beans
cauliflower florets
zucchini

Vegetarian Pâté

Geri Bleier, yogaview instructor

I can't stress how good this is. It looks and tastes exactly like chopped liver straight from a great Jewish deli. —Vivian

Preparation time: 20 minutes
Total time: 3 hours or more
Serves 4

1 can drained garden green peas
1 can drained chickpeas
¼ cup vegetable oil (or more if needed)
2-3 onions, chopped

⅔ cup walnuts
2 hard-boiled eggs, chopped (optional—
  omit to make vegan)
Salt and pepper to taste

Heat oil in sauté pan and add the onions. Lower heat and cook onions until slightly golden (about 10 minutes).

Briefly pulse green peas, chickpeas, and walnuts in food processor, then add onion and oil and continue to pulse until just blended (do not puree). Add salt and pepper to taste. Refrigerate several hours or overnight before serving.

Garnish with eggs. Serve with crackers or toast.

Corn Salsa

Claire Mark, yogaview instructor

This side salad is a fresh alternative to tomato salsa—you can also refrigerate any leftovers and use them on your salad the next day. —Claire

Preparation time: 30 minutes
Total time: 30 minutes
Serves 2-4

3-4 ears of corn
½ pint cherry tomatoes, chopped
¼ red onion, minced
juice of 1 lime

2 tablespoons of olive oil
a handful of cilantro, minced
salt to taste

Clean ears of corn while you boil a large pot of water. When water boils, place ears of corn inside pot and boil for 8 minutes, timed, then remove corn from pot and let cool for several minutes.

Over a bowl, use a knife to cut the corn away from the cob. Mix the rest of the ingredients with the corn and serve as a side, or with tortilla chips as an appetizer.

Hummus

Carole Mark, friend of yogaview

This recipe can be used as an appetizer served with fresh veggies and chips or as a spread for sandwiches. Garbanzo beans are naturally low in fat and high in fiber, making them heart healthy too! —Carole

Preparation time: 20 minutes
Total time: 20 minutes
Serves 6

1 cup of garbanzo beans (canned, or see
   directions below to make your own)
1 bay leaf
3-4 tablespoons of tahini
1 teaspoon cumin
½ teaspoon salt
zest of 1 lemon

2 lemons
2 garlic cloves
½ cup olive oil
Optional ingredients: parsley, a pinch
   of cayenne to make it more spicy, or
   roasted red peppers--all should be
   added in the food processor phase

To make your own beans, use 1 cup dried organic garbanzos soaked overnight. Once soaked, drain the beans, rinse them, cover with water, add 1 bag of chamomile tea and 1 bay leaf and simmer until beans are tender (at least ½ hour).

Remove bay leaf and tea bag. Place drained beans, tahini, cumin, salt, lemon zest, lemon juice, garlic, and other optional ingredients in the food processor.

While mixing, drizzle in olive oil.

Blend until smooth, adding water if needed to make it smoother.

Creamy Baba Ganoush

Claire Mark, yogaview instructor

This easy recipe uses a blender so the baba ganoush comes out creamy and delicious! It calls for roasted garlic so you may as well roast a head of garlic at the same time that you're cooking the eggplant (see page 70 for Roasted Garlic recipe). —Claire

Preparation time: 5 minutes
Total time: 1 hour 15 minutes
Serves 6 to 8 (as an appetizer)

1 eggplant
4 cloves roasted garlic
⅓ cup lemon juice
½ cup tahini

1 teaspoon cumin
2 tablespoon olive oil
½ teaspoon salt

Preheat the oven to 400°. Slice the ends off the eggplant, cut it lengthwise down the middle, place it cut face up on a baking sheet, and put it in the oven.

Squeeze 1½ fresh lemons (which should make 1/3 of a cup of lemon juice).

When the eggplant is very brown on top (about an hour) take it out of the oven and let it cool. Once it's cool, scrape out the inside of the eggplant and put the skin aside.

Combine the eggplant, garlic cloves, lemon juice, cumin, olive oil, and salt in a blender and blend until smooth.

Serve immediately!

Tabbouleh

Patrick Sarb, yogaview student

This is my version of my family's tabbouleh recipe. My mother is part Lebanese, and tabbouleh was always a fixture at our family gatherings--often several branches of the family would bring their own versions and we would compare and contrast. It is a fantastic, inexpensive meal that is not only healthy but easily adaptable to fit various dietary restrictions. You can easily substitute quinoa for the bulgur if you have a wheat allergy. It lasts up to five days in the fridge, and is great cold or at room temperature as either a side dish or the main meal. Using the best quality olive oil you can makes a big difference in the flavor of the salad. —Patrick

1 cup bulgur wheat, fine ground
2 cups hot tap water
3 bunches of Italian parsley, rinsed and finely chopped
1 bunch fresh mint, leaves rinsed and finely chopped
1 lb. tomatoes, seeded and chopped
2 cucumbers, peeled, seeded, and chopped

1 bunch scallions, rinsed, white and green part finely chopped
2 lemons, juiced
¼ cup good quality olive oil, plus 3 more tablespoons, separated
½ teaspoon cumin, ground
1 teaspoon salt
1-2 teaspoons pepper

In a large bowl, cover the bulgur wheat with hot water and let sit for 30 minutes. In the meantime, prepare and combine parsley, mint, tomatoes, cucumbers, and scallions in a large mixing bowl. Add juice of 1 and 1/2 lemons, ¼ cup olive oil, cumin, salt, and pepper. Mix ingredients and taste for seasoning.

In a fine mesh strainer, push the water out of the bulgur wheat, add to the vegetables, and stir to combine. Add remaining olive oil and lemon juice and toss once more. Taste for seasoning and add more salt and pepper as necessary. Allow flavors to meld for at least 30 minutes in the fridge before serving.

Tzatziki

Vivian Roumboulas, yogaview student

Tzatziki is a simple but delicious Greek yogurt and cucumber dip that can be used as a salad dressing, a dip for vegetables, a healthy substitute for mayonnaise on sandwiches, or just enjoyed on its own with pita bread as an appetizer or snack. —Vivian

Preparation time: 20 minutes
Total time: minimum 2½ hours
Serves 4

1 large (17 oz.) container Fage Greek yogurt, plain (2% or whole milk, do not use the fat free)
2 large garlic cloves, put through a press
juice of half a lemon
2 tablespoons white vinegar

½ hothouse cucumber, peeled and grated
¼-½ cup olive oil (reserve several tablespoons for drizzling over the top at serving)
salt and fresh black pepper

Mix all ingredients together and let stand in refrigerator for at least two hours and up to two days before serving.

Serve as a dip or a condiment.

A GALLERY OF GUACAMOLE

We can't say enough good things about guacamole and avocados! Avocados are nutritional powerhouses: they contain vitamins A, C, E, K and B6, as well as riboflavin, niacin, folate, and pantothenic acid. Rich in potassium and fiber, avocados are anti-inflammatory, antioxidant, and great for heart and skin health. They help regulate blood sugar and help you absorb all the other nutrients in your food. And best of all they're delicious!

We couldn't choose just one guac recipe so here are three different ones for you to experiment with.

Guacamole tips from our recipe writers:

Great guacamole is all about using perfectly ripe avocados. A ripe avocado is relatively firm, but will yield to gentle pressure when squeezed.

All of these recipes call for mixing your guac with a fork—do not use a food processor or overmix your guac. Good guacamole should be slightly lumpy in texture rather than creamy.

Guacamole should be served at room temperature. Try serving your guac with chips that have been heated in a 350° oven for 10 minutes. To preserve the color of your guacamole and make transporting it a snap, smooth the surface of the guac, squeeze additional lime juice on top, and then create an airtight seal with plastic wrap directly on the surface.

Basic Guacamole

Claire Mark, yogaview instructor

Preparation time: 15 minutes
Total time: 15 minutes
Serves 4

4 avocados, peeled and mashed with a fork
2 garlic cloves, minced
¼ red onion, minced
¼ cup cilantro, minced

1 to 2 limes, juiced
1 teaspoon of olive oil
salt to taste

Mix all of the above ingredients in a bowl and serve.

Guacamole with Mango and Tomatillo

Emily Kallemeyn, friend of yogaview

Preparation time: 20 minutes
Total time: 20 minutes
Serves 8-10

5 avocados, diced
1 ripe mango, diced
½ bunch cilantro, stems removed,
   fine chopped
¼ large red onion, fine chopped

3 tomatillos, chopped
½ jalapeño, seeds and stem removed,
   fine chopped
juice of 1 large lime
salt to taste

Set aside a spoonful of the diced mango, and stir the rest of the ingredients together with a fork. Scatter remaining mango over the top for garnish and color.

Spicy, Smoky, Garlicky Guacamole

Patrick Sarb, yogaview student

Preparation time: 20 minutes
Total time: 20 minutes
Serves 4-6

4 avocados
2 roma tomatoes, seeded and chopped
½ red onion, finely chopped
4 cloves of garlic, finely minced
3 limes
1 cup chopped cilantro leaves

1 serrano chile, seeded and minced (or
   jalapeño for milder heat)
½ teaspoon salt
¼ teaspoon freshly ground pepper
¼ teaspoon chipotle powder
¼ teaspoon cumin
4 dashes hot sauce

In a medium bowl, combine tomatoes, onion, and garlic with juice of one lime and a pinch of salt. Toss to allow garlic and onion to infuse the juice and flavor the tomatoes.

Halve and remove pits from avocados. Cut a crisscoss pattern in the flesh of the avocado. Use a spoon to scoop the avocado flesh into a large glass bowl, and douse with remaining lime juice. Mash avocado till just before your desired consistency.

Add tomato mixture, cilantro, salt, pepper, chipotle, cumin, and hot sauce. Stir to combine. Enjoy with your favorite tortilla chips.

Black Bean Salsa

Jennifer Boeder, yogaview instructor

My mother's salsa is the go-to dish that I bring to every potluck and gathering—it is easy to prepare, tasty, and very popular at parties! Use a combination of red, yellow, orange, and heirloom tomatoes to make it colorful; subtract the goat cheese to make it vegan. —Jennifer

Preparation time: 20 minutes
Total time: 20 minutes
Serves 6

2 cans black beans, rinsed and drained
1 can corn, drained
2 avocados, diced
1 red onion, diced
2 tomatoes, diced
a handful of fresh cilantro, minced

1 teaspoon cumin (or more to taste)
4 oz. (one small container) goat cheese
6 tablespoons fresh lime juice
6 tablespoons olive oil
sea salt to taste

After rinsing, combine black beans with the corn in a bowl. Add the diced avocado, red onion, and tomatoes. Mix in cilantro, lime juice, olive oil, and then add sea salt to taste (taste it with same chips you plan to serve it with—that way you'll be sure not to oversalt). This mixture can be covered and refrigerated for up to a day; when ready to eat, sprinkle a layer of goat cheese over the very top and serve with your favorite tortilla chips. Continue to top off the salsa with goat cheese as it gets eaten.

Pico de Gallo

Claire Mark, yogaview instructor

You can use any tomatoes in this recipe but try to use the freshest, brightest tomatoes you can find. Having a good tomato for pico de gallo makes all the difference! —Claire

Preparation time: 15 minutes
Total time: 15 minutes
Serves 6 to 8

5 vine-ripe bright red tomatoes
¼ cup red onion, diced
1 serrano chile, diced

⅛ cup cilantro, finely chopped
juice of 1 lime
¼ teaspoon of salt

Cut the tomatoes into small pieces and place in a colander with small holes over a bowl to drain all excess juices. Once juice has drained, add the red onion, diced chile, chopped cilantro, lime juice, and salt. Mix well and serve.

Carrot French Fries

Claire Mark, yogaview instructor

I called these carrot French fries because if you cook them long enough they get crispy on the edges and almost taste like a potato French fry ... only so much better for you! Serve with Portobello Mushroom Burgers at your next barbecue (see recipe page 104). —Claire

Preparation time: 10 minutes
Total time: 75-80 minutes
Serves 2 to 4

12 to 16 medium-sized carrots
2 tablespoons olive oil

½ teaspoon salt
black pepper to taste

Preheat the oven to 425°.

Peel the carrots and then cut them down to French-fry sized pieces. Coat with olive oil, salt, and pepper, mixing well to make sure they are coated evenly. Spread them out evenly on a baking sheet and place them in the oven.

After about 35 to 40 minutes mix them around a bit, but make sure that they are not overlapping when you put them back in the oven. Continue to bake until golden brown on the edges, about another 30 to 40 minutes. Remove from oven and eat warm!

Rosemary Roasted Potatoes

Claire Mark, yogaview instructor

While traveling in Italy, I had roasted potatoes that were so good I tried my best to replicate the recipe when I got home. The hardest part is not touching the potatoes once you put them in the oven! —Claire

Preparation time: 5 minutes
Total time: 95 minutes
Serves 4

12 small red potatoes, cut into 4-6 pieces each (depending on size)
4 to 6 cloves whole garlic, peeled

2 stalks rosemary, de-stemmed
⅓ cup olive oil
¼ teaspoon salt

Preheat the oven to 350°. Place the potatoes and whole garlic cloves on a baking sheet, pour the olive oil and salt on top, and mix well so that all the potatoes are coated in olive oil and salt. Sprinkle the rosemary on top and put sheet in oven.

Cook potatoes for 90 minutes, not touching them at all. You can lift and move the baking sheet around so that any excess olive oil continues to coat the bottom of the potatoes. The potatoes should be golden brown when done cooking. Remove from oven and serve.

Mashed Potatoes

Claire Mark, yogaview instructor

Adding the chives at the end gives these potatoes an extra fresh taste and brings some color in as well. —Claire

Preparation time: 5 minutes
Total time: 30 minutes
Serves 8

4 large Yukon Gold potatoes, skin on,
   cut into 6 pieces each
½ cup sour cream
½ cup whole milk

½ teaspoon salt (or more to taste)
2 tablespoons butter
1 to 2 tablespoons chives,
   finely chopped

Bring a large pot of water to boil. Add the cut potatoes to the water and cook for about 15 minutes (or until potatoes are soft enough to fall apart when poked with a fork).

Drain water from potatoes, then place potatoes, sour cream, milk, butter, and salt in a large bowl and mix well until all the lumps are out (I use a hand masher). Once the potatoes are mixed well, add the fresh chives and serve warm.

Sauteéd Greens

Claire Mark, yogaview instructor

The greens wilt down a lot, so a few bunches could end up being a side dish for 2 to 4 people, depending on how much they like greens! —Claire

Preparation time: 20 minutes
Total time: 30 minutes
Serves 2-4

1 bunch greens (kale, collard, beet greens, or chard)
1 or 2 garlic cloves minced (depends on how much you like garlic)

2 tablespoons olive oil
sea salt
black pepper (or crushed hot peppers if you like your greens spicy)

Trim hard stalks from center of greens and cut remaining leaves into bite-sized pieces (remember greens will wilt down, so don't make the pieces too small—2 inches by 2 inches is good).

Wash cut greens thoroughly in cold water (I like to fill my sink with water and let them sit there for a bit to clean them well).

Preheat a skillet on the stove, medium high heat. Add 1 tablespoon of oil; when it's hot, add minced garlic.

When the garlic is just starting to brown, add all the greens to the skillet. Sprinkle with a little salt and either black pepper or crushed hot peppers. Add second tablespoon of oil if greens look dry.

Stir occasionally until wilted but still green. Serve warm.

Roasted Broccoli

Claire Mark, yogaview instructor

This recipe has become a weekly staple of my diet—it's quick, easy, and ideal for times when you know you need to eat something green but lack the energy to chop a ton of vegetables. —Jennifer

Preparation time: 10 minutes
Total time: 25 minutes
Serves 4

2 heads broccoli, broken up into florets
3 garlic cloves, minced
1 shallot, minced

1 pint cherry tomatoes, whole
3 tablespoons olive oil
1 teaspoon hot pepper flakes

Toss all the ingredients in a bowl (see photo), then put broccoli florets on a sheet pan and roast in oven at 425° for about 15 minutes (until florets are slightly browned and crispy). Serve warm.

Roasted Cauliflower with Tahini and Date Syrup

Vivian Roumboulas, yogaview student

You can find date syrup online or at Middle Eastern markets--totally worth seeking out for its unique flavor. —Vivian

Preparation time: 10 minutes
Total time: 30 minutes
Serves 4

One head cauliflower
¼ cup tahini (or more to taste)
¼ cup date syrup (or substitute dark honey)
2-3 tablespoons olive oil

2 teaspoons each lemon juice and lemon
    zest (zest is optional, but brightens
    the dish)
sea salt and freshly ground pepper

Preheat oven to 425°. Break cauliflower up into florets. Toss with olive oil and season with salt and pepper. Spread cauliflower on baking sheet in single layer.

Roast in oven until edges begin to brown and cauliflower releases nutty, roasted aroma (about 20 minutes).

Remove from oven and spread on serving plate. Drizzle with tahini and date syrup, sprinkle lemon juice and zest on top, and serve.

Roasted Asparagus

Claire Mark, yogaview instructor

Wild asparagus were used in ancient Greece and Rome as an herbal remedy to flush the kidneys; asparagus contain folic acid and are a good source of antioxidants. —Claire

Preparation time: 10 minutes
Total time: 30 minutes
Serves 4

16 asparagus stalks
¼ cup olive oil
salt and black pepper to taste

Preheat oven to 425° degrees. Trim bottom part of asparagus that snaps off easily. Rinse asparagus in cool water and lay on baking sheet. Pour olive oil on top and sprinkle with salt and black pepper.

Mix until asparagus are evenly coated; be sure not to let asparagus overlap on baking sheet. Place in oven and let roast until brown on edges (approximately 20 minutes depending on your oven).

Serve immediately, or refrigerate and add to salad the following day!

Roasted Garlic

Claire Mark, yogaview instructor

Garlic has been used throughout recorded history for both medicinal and culinary purposes (the ancient Greeks would feed garlic to their athletes before they competed in the Olympic games). Packed with antioxidants and vitamins, it's great for your immune system and heart health. This recipe is an easy way to bring more garlic into your diet, and when mixed with olive oil and Parmesan cheese is a perfect topping for any toasted bread. You can also add it to salad dressings, hummus, or drizzle over steamed vegetables. —Jennifer

Preparation time: 5 minutes
Cooking time: 1 hour
Serves 4 to 6

1 head garlic
1 teaspoon olive oil

Preheat the oven to 400°.

Peel the outer layer of skin off the garlic, cut the top pointy ends off, and put the garlic in tin foil.

Pour the olive oil over the exposed parts of the garlic, close the tin foil around the top and put it in the oven. After 45 minutes, open the top of the tin foil and let bake for another 15 minutes. Remove from oven, let cool, and squeeze out garlic cloves to use as spread. Keeps for about 7-10 days in an airtight container in the refrigerator; freeze for up to 3 months.

Szechwan Beans

Carole Mark, friend of yogaview

Chinese long beans make this recipe crisp and visually more interesting. I tried to have one serving, and kept going back for more … it's addictive. —Vivian

Preparation time: 20 minutes
Total time: 20 minutes
Serves 4

1 pound Chinese long beans (also called yardlong beans or just long beans)
1 tablespoon garlic, chopped
1 tablespoon ginger, chopped
2 stalks scallions, white parts only
¼ teaspoon chili flakes or chili paste
2 tablespoons sesame seeds

1 tablespoon dark soy sauce
½ teaspoon sugar
¼ teaspoon salt, or to taste
pepper to taste (optional)
1 tablespoon sesame oil
2 tablespoons vegetable or peanut oil for stir-frying, or more as needed

Wash the long beans, drain thoroughly, and trim the tops and bottoms. Cut into 3-4 inch segments. Mix the soy sauce, sugar, salt, optional pepper, and sesame oil and set aside. Chop the garlic, ginger, and white part of the scallions and set aside.

Blanch beans for 1-2 minutes in boiling water, then transfer them to a container of ice water, leave for a minute, then drain.

Heat 1 tablespoon peanut oil in a pan or wok over medium heat. Add the long beans and sesame seeds and stir-fry until they start to brown (3-5 minutes.) Remove the long beans, drain excess oil, and set aside.

Heat 1 tablespoon oil in the same pan or wok on medium-high heat. Add the garlic, ginger, and scallions. Stir-fry for a few seconds, then add the chili flakes and stir-fry for a few more seconds until aromatic. Add the longbeans and the remaining ingredients. Mix together and serve.

Greens Gomae

Carole Mark, friend of yogaview

This recipe calls for blanched greens (placing greens in boiling water for a minute or two until tender). Whether or not you prefer your blanched greens cooked all the way through, or al dente (meaning firm to the bite) is a personal preference. First, learn how to successfully blanch your vegetables all the way through, and then if you prefer them al dente, just back off on the blanching time a little bit.

Once the greens becomes tender and their color is intensified, remove from boiling water and immerse in ice water, which will cause them to cool rapidly and keeps them from overcooking. —Carole

Preparation time: 15 minutes
Total time: 15 minutes
Serves 4

For the greens:
10-12 oz. (two big bunches) greens:
  spinach, beet greens, Swiss chard,
  or kale (you may combine types of
  greens once you've blanched them)
2-3 tablespoons sesame seeds, toasted
  in dry pan until browned

For the sauce:
4 tablespoons tahini
1 tablespoon soy sauce
1 tablespoon sake or rice wine
½ tablespoon sugar

Wash greens. Boil a large pot of water and blanch greens in batches for 1 to 2 minutes depending on the tenderness of the greens (spinach will blanch extremely quickly, for example, whereas tougher greens like kale will take a minute or two).

Remove greens from water and run under cold water or plunge in ice water. Drain well, and squeeze out all excess water until greens are tightly packed.

Cut greens in block-shaped squares. Place blocks in shallow bowl and top with sauce and sesame seeds.

Fish Taco Coleslaw

Claire Mark, yogaview instructor

Although recommended for fish tacos (see recipe page 92) this coleslaw is also great on its own. —Claire

Preparation time: 15 minutes
Total time: 15 minutes
Serves 4-6

½ white cabbage sliced thinly into
   2-inch-long pieces
½ white onion, sliced thinly

juice of 1-2 limes
a handful of cilantro, minced
¼ cup olive oil

Mix ingredients and serve.

Cabbage and Carrot Coleslaw

Claire Mark, yogaview instructor

When it comes to antioxidant and cancer-fighting foods, cabbage ranks right up there with broccoli, cauliflower, and Brussels sprouts. It's also a great source of vitamin C, fiber, and potassium. —Claire

Preparation time: 15 minutes
Total time: 15 minutes
Serves 4-5

For the slaw:
½ large-sized cabbage (5-6 oz),
   chopped finely
2 orange carrots, sliced thin
2 purple carrots, sliced thin
   (if you can find them–if not,
   4 orange carrots will do)

For the dressing:
4 tablespoons olive oil
1 tablespoon apple cider vinegar
½ tablespoon Dijon mustard
½ tablespoon mayo
sea salt

Whisk together dressing ingredients. Toss cabbage and carrots with dressing, salt to taste, and serve.

Ceviche

Kenny Martell, friend of yogaview

Ceviche is an old tradition in South America, and every Central and South American nation has their own special version of the dish. The ancient Incas used fruit juice, salt, and chile peppers to preserve fresh fish; the citric acid in the juice "cooks" the fish, and the result is a light, refreshing appetizer or main course. —Kenny

Preparation time: 15 minutes
Total time: 2-3 hours (including marinating time)
Serves 6-8

2 lbs. of firm, fresh fish filets (tilapia, red snapper, or other firm-fleshed fish) cut into 1/8 pieces, completely deboned
¼ cup fresh squeezed lemon juice
¼ cup fresh squeezed red grapefruit
½ cup fresh squeezed orange juice
½ red onion, finely diced
1 cup tomatoes, finely diced

1 jalapeño pepper, seeded and finely diced (more if you wish the dish to be hotter)
1 cup chopped cilantro
salt to taste
tortilla chips or saltines for serving
Optional garnish: 1 cup diced avocado, 1 cup diced pineapple, 1 cup diced mango

Combine the citrus juices, pour them into a non-reactive casserole dish, and add raw fish.* Stir and let sit covered in the refrigerator for 1 hour, then stir again and let the fish marinate another 1-2 hours. Fish will change to a whiter color and become opaque.

Add the rest of the ingredients, stir and let sit for an additional 15 minutes. Salt to taste and garnish with optional mango, pineapple, or avocado.

For serving, you can place the ceviche in a large bowl and let people spoon it onto individual plates to eat with chips or saltines. Or, spoon the ceviche into sundae glasses, martini glasses, or small bowls. Garnish with sprigs of cilantro and slices of lime, and serve with tostadas, tortilla chips, or saltines.

* *If you are not comfortable with just marinating the raw fish in the citrus marinade, you can place fish in a large pot of water with salt and cook for 1 minute or 2 minutes maximum. Immediately remove and place into a bowl of ice water to stop the cooking, and then follow recipe as directed.*

You may also substitute cooked shrimp for the fish; place 2 lbs. small/medium-sized shrimp in a large pot of water with salt and cook for 1 minute or 2 minutes maximum. Immediately remove and place into a bowl of ice water to stop the cooking, then follow recipe as directed.

Zucchini Squares

Dee Davis, yogaview instructor

These zucchini squares are colorful, super easy, and will help you use up that summer zucchini. —Dee

Preparation time: 10 minutes
Total time: 1 hour
Serves 4-6

3 cups diced zucchini
½ cup chopped parsley
½ cup grated Parmesan cheese
½ cup diced onion
4 eggs, lightly beaten
1 cup organic baking mix or
  1 cup flour

1 ½ teaspoons baking powder
½ teaspoon salt
1 tablespoon butter
½ cup safflower oil
  (or other light cooking oil)
salt and pepper to taste

Pre-heat oven to 350°. Mix all ingredients together and pour into 8-inch square greased baking dish. Bake for 30-40 minutes, or until golden brown.

awareness

Anuvittasana—Standing Backbend Pose
Wicker Park

We all have moments of rushing or being on autopilot in the yoga studio and at the kitchen table. Taking a moment to pause, slow down, and be mindful will enhance both experiences and deepen our consciousness.

entrées

Breakfast for Dinner: Eggs

Claire Mark, yogaview instructor

This recipe is my healthy take on Eggs Benedict—great for those evenings when your kitchen inventory is low and you want a quick, savory homemade dinner. —Claire

Preparation time: 15 minutes
Total time: 15 minutes
Serves 2

2 slices sourdough bread
1 bunch of greens (collard, beet, or chard)
  washed, de-stemmed, and chopped
1 tablespoon olive oil

2 eggs
1 teaspoon butter
truffle oil (optional)
salt to taste

Heat a skillet and add olive oil. When olive oil is hot, add greens and cook until wilted but still green. Add salt to taste, remove from heat, and set aside.

In same skillet that greens were cooked, add butter, heat, and swirl it around to coat the pan.

Turn down the heat and crack an egg in the pan; let cook for 2 minutes and then flip, again cooking for 2 minutes.

While egg is cooking put toasted bread on plate, add greens on top, then add egg on top of greens when egg is done cooking (yoke should be wet but the white should be dry). Sprinkle with salt, add a drizzle of truffle oil, and serve warm.

To make with a poached egg instead of a fried egg:

Heat a 2.5 quart pot half full of water and add 2 tablespoons of white wine vinegar (this will help the whites of the egg stay together).

While water is heating, crack an egg in a small bowl and set aside.

Bring a pot of water to a near-boil (if the water is at a full boil it's too much).

When water is ready, gently drop egg into center of pot, without breaking the yolk. Keep water at near-boil.

Let egg cook for 4 minutes, timed, then remove with a slotted spoon. Add on top of greens and serve!

Breakfast for Dinner: Pancakes

Betty Newman, friend of yogaview

You can add your choice of fruits, nuts, and spices to the batter—we've suggested some here, but feel free to get creative with this recipe! —Jennifer

Preparation time: 25 minutes
Total time: 25 minutes
Serves 4

2 eggs
2 cups (or less) of buttermilk or
   almond milk
1 cup wheat or buckwheat flour
½ cup applesauce (in place of oil)
½ cup oatmeal
¼ cup wheat germ
1 teaspoon salt
1 teaspoon baking powder
2 tablespoons honey
2 tablespoons or more of olive oil,
   coconut oil, or cooking oil of your choice
   (you'll use this to cook the pancakes in)
maple syrup, date syrup, or honey (to
   dress the pancakes when serving)

Optional fruits/nuts/spices of your choice:
choose one of each from these lists or
add your own!

Nuts:
almonds, pecans, walnuts

Spices:
cardamom, cinnamon, nutmeg, vanilla

Fruits, dried or fresh:
apples, apricots, bananas, blueberries,
cranberries, strawberries

Chop your nuts and fruits into small pieces.

Beat eggs well. Gradually stir in 1 cup of milk, applesauce, nuts, fruits, spices, and all other dry ingredients.

Beat until smooth. Add remaining milk (less liquid will give you a thicker pancake and vice versa).

Cook over medium low heat, on lightly oiled skillet. Ladle 1/3 cup of batter per pancake onto heated skillet. Flip pancakes when they are puffed and full of bubbles.

Cook other side until golden brown. Keep the heat medium low, because of the honey they can burn quickly.

Serve warm with maple syrup, date syrup, or honey.

Spanakopita

Vivian Roumboulas, yogaview student

Spanakopita is a delicious savory pie made with spinach and feta cheese. This classic Greek entree will work as an appetizer, side dish, or even a light lunch. —Vivian

1 box frozen filo dough, thawed and kept in box until ready to use
2 lbs. frozen leaf spinach (do not use chopped spinach)
½-¾ lb. unsalted butter
1 large sweet onion, chopped and sautéed until softened
½ bunch fresh Italian leaf parsley
½ cup chopped fresh dill

1 bunch scallion chopped white and part of green
2 beaten eggs
¾ lb. feta cheese (purchase from deli, or packed in brine, do not use pre-crumbled)
¼ cup whole milk ricotta cheese
⅛ cup grated Parmesan cheese
salt and freshly ground pepper

Preheat oven to 350°. Melt butter, starting with ½ lb., and keep warm. Butter a 9" x 13" Pyrex dish, including the rim.

Allow the spinach to thaw enough to chop finely, then transfer to a colander to thaw completely. Take thawed spinach and wring out between paper towels to remove any excess water. Don't skip this step!

Take a clean dishtowel and wet it slightly. Wring out so it's just damp, and keep it handy for covering the filo dough that's not being used. (You can use damp paper towels as well.)

In large bowl, combine spinach, onion, herbs, scallion, and cheeses. Taste mixture and season with salt and pepper. Add beaten eggs and combine thoroughly. Carefully open filo and remove half the sheets.

Line pan with first sheet of filo, and use a pastry brush to butter the top with the melted butter. Repeat with each sheet of filo until half the package is used up. Keep the other half covered with damp dishtowel.

Carefully and evenly spoon spinach mix into pan.

Repeat filo process with remaining sheets to cover. Trim any excess from the edges of the pan and score the top to prevent the spanakopita from splitting in the oven.

Cook until golden brown on top (about 45 minutes to one hour). Serve warm or at room temperature, or refrigerate for up to 3-4 days.

Greek Briami

Paula Koutsouvas, friend of yogaview

Classic Greek dishes are all about delicious fresh vegetables, wonderful cheeses, and the love that goes into making a good meal. This is one of those family style recipes that is part of every ethnic cuisine—one that everyone's grandmother makes, but has never written down because she knows it by heart. One thing I have learned from my husband's grandmother, who is 97, is that when you think you have added enough olive oil to this dish, you should probably add a little bit more. It's also a very forgiving recipe—you can add or subtract whatever vegetables/spices you want, and it reheats well. —Paula

Preparation time: 10 minutes
Total time: 2 hours
Serves 6-8

12 small red potatoes
6 carrots
4 small eggplants
2 medium zucchinis
1 onion
3 cloves garlic

½ pound of peas
1 large can whole tomatoes and their
 juice or 4-5 tomatoes
⅔ to 1 cup olive oil (or more)
a handful of fresh or dried herbs—dill or
 an herbs de Provence mix will work

Leave potatoes and tomatoes whole; chop all other vegetables into large pieces. Cut the cloves of garlic in half.

Use as big a pan as possible to cook this dish--otherwise when the veggies get juicy, they can get soggy as opposed to roasting. Toss chopped vegetables (except peas, tomatoes, and fresh herbs) in a large pan with salt and black pepper, dried herbs (if using instead of fresh) and **lots** of olive oil (my rule is that when you think you have put in enough, put in some more). Generous amounts of olive oil are important for making the sauce so thick and tasty. I have tried to do it with less but the flavor just isn't as good.

Roast tossed vegetables at 425° degrees until the veggies have cooked down a bit and are starting to brown (about 1 hour).

Once vegetables start to brown, chop tomatoes (if using fresh) and add them to the pan, or add can of tomatoes. Continue to cook for another hour or so, stirring periodically. Add the peas and fresh herbs about 5-10 minutes before the end of cooking time. Once the mixture starts to thicken up and look more saucy, it's done.

Serve with chunks of feta cheese and crusty bread.

Spaghetti Squash

Claire Mark, yogaview instructor

Claire made this dish for one of our cookbook meetings, and immediately upon tasting it all of us insisted it be included in the book! It's an ideal cold-weather dish—I've probably made it ten times since then. It's the perfect wheat-free, gluten-free pasta. You can experiment with adding different types of cheeses, herbs, and flavoring to the squash (butter, goat cheese, chives, and truffle oil all taste fantastic) or just season with oil and herbs to make vegan. —Jennifer

Preparation time: 35-45 minutes
Total time: 55 minutes
Serves 2

1 spaghetti squash
¼ cup Parmesan cheese or cheese of
   your choice (more or less, to taste)
1 teaspoon olive oil (or more)

2 tablespoons basil, chopped
chili flakes (optional)
salt to taste

Preheat oven to 375°.

Cut spaghetti squash in half, lengthwise. Add ¼ inch of water to a casserole dish and put spaghetti squash in it, cut side down. Bake in oven for about 35-40 minutes.
Remove squash and place the two pieces cut side up on a plate.

Take a fork, and with the tines turned down, drag the fork over the flesh of the squash, pulling towards you—the squash should separate into thin threads like spaghetti! Repeat this scraping process until you've separated all the squash into threads. Add the olive oil, Parmesan cheese, basil, and chili flakes and mix in. You can eat this dish right out of the squash rind, or transfer to a plate.

Serve hot!

Spicy Peanut Pasta

Tiffin Kearney Bolger, friend of yogaview

I love entrees with peanut sauce but often avoid them in an effort to eat lighter. In this recipe I have drastically reduced calories by using sherry and veggie broth in the dressing rather than the oil that is typically the binder. I also used wheat noodles to boost the nutrition. I love the versatility of this dish—you can serve it hot, room temperature, or cold. It even freezes well. The dressing can be made in advance and refrigerated until you are ready to use it. For a spicier version, just add more hot sauce! —Tiffin

Preparation time: 40 minutes
Total time: 40 minutes
Serves 4

24 oz. whole wheat thin spaghetti
2 tablespoons sesame or olive oil
1 bunch of cilantro, roughly chopped
6 whole green onions, thinly sliced

Peanut dressing:
5 cloves garlic
1 cup peanut butter
¾ cups soy sauce
1 tablespoon fresh grated ginger

4 tablespoons rice vinegar
6 tablespoons brown sugar
1 tablespoons Sriracha sauce
  (a.k.a. "rooster sauce")
¼ cup sherry
¼ cup vegetable broth

For garnish: chopped peanuts and
  cilantro (optional)

Fill a large pot with water and bring it to a boil. Add spaghetti and reduce to simmer. (Dry spaghetti takes about 10 minutes to cook, but some brands take less and some take more. Check the package to see how long your spaghetti requires.)

Once cooked, drain spaghetti and toss with 2 tablespoons sesame oil.

Blend all peanut dressing ingredients in blender or food processor. Chill until ready to use.

Combine noodles, sauce, green onions, and cilantro. Garnish with more cilantro and chopped peanuts if desired. You can serve this salad warm, cold, or room temperature.

Daal

Tamiz Haiderali, Township Restaurant

This is a simple, healthy, and hearty meal. The recipe can be altered by adding other spices and garnishes, and can be prepared vegan. One can add vegetables such as squashes, zucchinis, spinach--or just eat it by itself. It can be served as soup (by adding vegetable broth) or served with basmati rice, naan, or a crusty bread. —Tamiz

Preparation time: 45 minutes
Total time: 55 minutes
Serves 6

Part One:
1 cup lentils (pink/masoor daal) rinsed
  (wash in sieve until water runs clear)
4 cups water
1 tablespoon garlic, minced
½ tablespoon ginger, minced
1 teaspoon salt

Part Two:
2 tablespoons oil (grapeseed, safflower,
  or other vegetable oil) or butter, or a
  combination of the two

½ tablespoon chopped garlic (or less,
  if you aren't a garlic lover like me)
1 teaspoon chopped ginger
½ teaspoon cayenne
⅛ teaspoon turmeric
1 teaspoon cumin powder
1 teaspoon coriander powder
2 teaspoons cumin seeds
juice of 1 lemon (optional)
1 onion, finely diced
1 tomato, finely diced (optional)
For the garnish: fresh chopped cilantro
  and mint (optional)

Bring all ingredients in Part One to a boil, removing and discarding all the foam that floats at the top (scoop it off at least twice). After about 15 minutes, the consistency of the lentils should be soft and easy to break with a stirring spoon. When soft, mash the lentils just slightly, but do not puree them.

Meanwhile, heat a separate pan (preferably non-stick) and when hot, add oil and/or butter. When oil is hot, add onions and sweat, stirring often, until translucent. Add cumin seeds and stir for 30 seconds.

When cumin crackles and gives off a slight aroma, add garlic and ginger and continue to stir. When garlic starts to take on a slight reddish-brown color, turn off heat and add remaining spices. Stir well for 30 seconds. Avoid letting spices stick to the pan. Add lemon juice. If using tomatoes, add them and leave heat on, letting them simmer for 5 minutes or until tomatoes are soft, stirring frequently. Toss the spice mixture into the softened lentils. Let mixture simmer for 10 minutes. Taste for salt.

Serve with a fresh chopped cilantro and mint garnish (optional) atop basmati rice, naan, or a crusty bread.

Coconut Curried Kale with Soba Noodles

AJ Durand and Emily Kallemeyn, yogaview teacher/friend of yogaview

This dish is great served cold as well as hot—simply subtract the fish sauce to make vegan. —Jennifer

Preparation time: 20 minutes
Total time: 20 minutes
Serves 4-6

1-2 bunch(es) green kale (enough to fill a large pot raw)
1 can regular coconut milk
1 tablespoon green curry paste (or more to taste)
1 tablespoon freshly grated ginger
2 cloves garlic, minced
1-2 tablespoons fish sauce (optional—if making vegan, add 1/2 cup of white onion, finely chopped, and salt to taste)

1 tablespoon brown sugar
1 small can sliced water chestnuts, drained and rinsed
1 cup chopped or sliced unsalted almonds
8 oz. (1 package) soba noodles (I like the ones made with yams)
1 tablespoon toasted sesame oil
½ cup olive oil or hemp oil
½ cup flax seed
salt to taste

Set a full kettle of water to boil. While the water heats, tear the kale from the spine, rinse, and place in a large pot with a steamer tray and just enough water to fill to the steamer line. Cover and steam at medium heat for 5 minutes or until the kale is bright green (leaves should soften but still be firm). In a medium saucepan, heat a tablespoon of olive oil, then sauté the ginger and garlic (add the onion at this stage if preparing vegan) for 2-3 minutes (or until the garlic begins to brown). Add the coconut milk, curry paste, sugar, and optional fish sauce and simmer on low, stirring occasionally.

Place the soba noodles in a large bowl (you may need to break them). When the kettle whistles, pour the boiling water over the noodles and cover the bowl with a plate for about 10 minutes.

Remove the kale from the steamer, rinse the pot, and return the kale. Cover with coconut curry concoction, add almonds and water chestnuts and toss (careful, it's hot!).

Drain the soba noodles and return them to the bowl. Add sesame oil and the rest of the olive oil and toss with flax seed.

Add equal amounts of kale and soba to the same bowl, salt to taste, and serve.

Vegetable Stir Fry with Soy Peanut Sauce

Valerie Bolon, yogaview student

This recipe can be made with any desired vegetables and the spiciness can easily be increased or decreased. A simple way to add more vegetables to your diet! —Valerie

½ onion, diced
½ bell pepper
1 carrot, peeled and diced
1 tomato, cored and diced
½ cup broccoli, cut into small florettes
½ cup mushrooms, chopped
4 pieces bok choy, rinsed and cut
   lengthwise into quarters
1 teaspoon ginger, peeled and minced
1 teaspoon garlic, peeled and minced
¼ cup peanuts, rough chopped

1 cup peanut butter
¼ cup soy sauce
1 tablespoon fish sauce
1 tablespoon sambal or any chili sauce or
   flakes (use less for less spiciness)
¼ cup rice vinegar
½ cup water
¼ cup lime juice
1-2 tablespoons cooking oil
1-2 scallions, thinly chopped (for garnish)

Place a large sauté pan over medium heat. Heat the pan for about a minute, then add cooking oil. Add onion and sauté 2-3 minutes until onions are translucent. Add remaining vegetables (bell pepper, carrot, broccoli, tomato, bok choy, ginger, and garlic).

Sauté all vegetables together for about 5 minutes, stirring occasionally. While the vegetables are cooking, mix remaining ingredients in a bowl with a whisk: peanut butter, rice vinegar, soy sauce, fish sauce, sambal (or whatever chili spice desired), lime juice, and water. The mixture should be pourable.

Pour sauce into the sauté pan to completely cover the vegetables. Let the sauce cook with the vegetables about 2-3 minutes. Taste to ensure it has the desired flavor and spiciness. Add peanuts and chopped scallions to garnish. Serve over rice.

Roasted Brussels Sprouts with Cashews and Cranberries

Erica Merrill & Mike Morgan, yogaview instructor/yogaview student

Erica is another one of yogaview's many brilliant kitchen MacGyvers—she improvised this recipe one night based on leftovers in her fridge, and it was so delicious it I made it again in our friend Mike Morgan's kitchen. He added the fresh herbs as well as roasting the vegetables cut side down in oil for maximum crispiness. —Jennifer

Preparation time: 20 minutes
Total time: 30 minutes
Serves 4

16 oz. (one bag) Brussels sprouts, rinsed, brown ends trimmed
16 oz. fingerling or new potatoes
1 cup dried cranberries
½ cup cashews
½ cup pine nuts
½ cup sunflower seeds

¾ cup olive oil (or more as needed)
juice of 1 lemon
3-4 stalks fresh rosemary
  (or 2 teaspoons dried)
3-4 stalks fresh thyme
  (or 2 teaspoons dried)
sea salt and pepper to taste

Preheat oven to 425°. Lightly drizzle two sheet pans with about ¼ a cup of the olive oil. If using fresh herbs, strip rosemary needles and thyme sprigs from the stalks, chop lightly, and set aside.

Rinse potatoes, cut them in half, place in a bowl, and toss with ¼ cup olive oil, chopped herbs, salt, and pepper. Place potatoes cut side down on one sheet pan, and then place pan in oven. (Potatoes should precede the Brussels sprouts in the oven by five minutes, as they will take longer to cook.)

Cut Brussels sprouts in half and toss with last ¼ cup of olive oil, salt, and pepper, then place them cut sides down on the second sheet pan (save any loose leaves that fall off the sprouts and scatter them on the pan as well). Put Brussels sprouts in the oven, and while vegetables are roasting, rough chop cashews and toast pine nuts over low heat in a small pan on stove (keep an eye on them as they can burn quickly!) Potatoes should roast 15-20 minutes or until browned; Brussels sprouts should roast 10-15 minutes or until browned and crispy.

When vegetables are done roasting, remove sheet pans from oven and mix potatoes and Brussels sprouts in a bowl with cashews, pinenuts, sunflower seeds, lemon juice, and cranberries. Add salt, pepper, and oil if needed to taste; serve warm.

Colorful Quinoa

Maria Rosner, yogaview instructor

As a vegetarian, I'm always looking for new ways beyond beans and tofu to get adequate protein. Quinoa is a great alternative that is easy to prepare and endlessly versatile. I created this salad one summer for a dinner party of non-vegetarians, and everyone loved it! My secret ingredient: Eros Pista pepper spread from Hungary, which I now order online. If you can find it, substitute for the Tabasco. —Maria

Preparation time: 25 minutes
Total time: 25 minutes
Serves 4-6

1 cup uncooked black or red quinoa
2 cups water or vegetable stock
½ red pepper, diced
½ yellow pepper, diced
1 ripe avocado, cubed
½ red onion (or less, to taste), chopped fine
1 bunch fresh cilantro, chopped fine

For the dressing:
2 tablespoons olive oil
¼ cup red wine vinegar (or to taste)
sea salt to taste
dash of Eros Pista pepper spread or Tabasco

Rinse quinoa thoroughly (do not skip this step). Add quinoa and water or stock to a saucepan and bring to a boil, then reduce heat and cook for 20 minutes (or until all water is absorbed). Transfer cooked quinoa to a salad bowl and allow to cool completely.

Add peppers, avocado, and cilantro. Add red onion slowly, to taste (depending upon how much you enjoy raw onion!) Mix lightly.

Mix dressing ingredients and pour over salad, just before serving. Toss well and enjoy!

Spicy Fish Tacos
Claire Mark, yogaview instructor

I love fish tacos, but wanted to create a healthier version where the fish was baked instead of fried. —Claire

Preparation time: 30 minutes
Total time: 35 minutes
Serves 4 (8 tacos total)

For the tacos:
2 tilapia fillets
8 corn tortillas
1-2 limes, juiced
2 avocados, sliced
1 tablespoon olive oil

½ tablespoon cumin
½ tablespoon paprika
salt and pepper to taste
Fish Taco Coleslaw (see recipe page 74)
chipotle mayonnaise
    (you can use store bought, or see
    recipe below)

Preheat oven to 350°. Place fish in a baking dish and lightly coat with olive oil and lime juice. Sprinkle fish with cumin, salt, paprika, and pepper. Place fish in oven and heat until fish is flaky and white, and no longer opaque (about 10 minutes).

While fish is cooking, heat corn tortillas on skillet with a small amount of olive oil. Remove fish from oven and flake it into small pieces. Place corn tortillas on plate and add chipotle mayo, fish, coleslaw, avocado, and fresh cilantro—serve warm.

For the chipotle mayo:
8 oz. good quality mayonnaise
1 small can chipotle chilies in adobo
½ teaspoon cumin
juice of 1 lime (or more to taste)

Place mayonnaise in blender, food processor, or mixing bowl.

Take 2 tablespoons of the adobo from can of chilies and add to bowl, with one of the chopped chilies. Add cumin and lime. Blend thoroughly. Taste and adjust heat to taste by adding more chilies or adobo.

Sautéed Tilapia With Lemon Caper Sauce

Amy Schatz, yogaview instructor

I made this recipe several times, varying the type of capers and tomatoes I used. In late summer, I used multicolor grape/cherry tomatoes. This dish bursts with tart/sweet flavors--I love making it when I have a small dinner get-together. —Vivian

Preparation time: 30 minutes
Total time: 30 minutes
Serves 4

½ cup flour
12 oz. tilapia (3 4-oz. fillets)
⅓ cup dry white wine
16 oz. fresh spinach
½ small lemon (for dressing spinach)
¼ cup capers (nonpareil, small)
1 cup grape or cherry tomatoes,
   halved or quartered depending on size

4 tablespoons butter
   (divided, 1 tablespoon cold)
2 tablespoons grapeseed oil
2 garlic cloves, minced
juice of 1-2 small lemons, zest reserved
1 teaspoon fresh thyme
salt and freshly ground pepper to taste

For the fish:
Dredge fish fillets in flour seasoned with salt and pepper, tap to remove excess and set aside. Heat 1 tablespoon butter and 2 tablespoons grapeseed oil in large sauté pan over medium high heat. Once butter melts, turn heat down to medium, place fish in hot pan and cook 2 minutes per side, or until fish is a light golden brown. Remove fillets and tent with foil until all fillets are cooked.

For the spinach:
Heat 1 tablespoon butter in pan over medium heat. Add spinach and cook, stirring constantly for one minute until just wilted. Squeeze lemon juice over top of spinach to taste, or just drizzle with a little olive oil. Season with salt and pepper.

For the sauce:
Heat 1 tablespoon butter in pan over medium heat and add garlic. Once garlic is fragrant and softened, add white wine, turn up heat, and allow to reduce slightly. Add lemon juice, lemon zest, thyme, and capers. Stir over medium-low heat for 2-3 minutes. Add tomatoes, stirring just to cover with sauce, and then remove from heat. Take final tablespoon of butter and whisk in to thicken sauce just before serving.

Spread spinach over bottom of each serving plate, top with fish fillet, and spoon sauce over top.

Rainbow Trout With Lime and Brown Butter

Vivian Roumboulas, yogaview student

Trout is another excellent source of both protein and omega-3 fatty acids, as well as vitamin B12, vitamin B6, niacin, potassium, phosphorus, and selenium. —Vivian

Preparation time: 10 minutes
Total time: 10 minutes
Serves 4

1 lb. fresh rainbow trout fillets with skin
1 tablespoon grapeseed oil
juice of 2 limes
½ cup slivered almonds, toasted until slightly browned

¼ cup each, chopped Italian parsley and cilantro
4 tablespoons unsalted butter
salt and freshly ground pepper

Preheat oven to 400°.

Take trout fillets and season them generously with salt and pepper on both sides.
In cast iron skillet, heat grapeseed oil until **very** hot over high heat.

Add trout, skin side down and allow the skin to crisp, approximately 2-3 minutes.
Using a fish spatula, and taking care not to rip the skin, flip trout fillets. After 1-2 minutes, turn heat down to medium high.

Meanwhile in a stainless steel sauté pan or small saucepan, add butter and heat over medium high heat, watching carefully until it turns dark brown and has a nutty but not burnt aroma. Immediately remove from heat and place in a cool ceramic bowl so that it doesn't continue to brown and set aside.

Remove trout from stovetop and place in preheated oven.

Trout should be done in 3-5 minutes, depending on thickness. **Do not overcook.**
Remove from oven and pour lime juice over fish, serving crispy skin side up.

Top with almonds and chopped herbs. Finish by pouring brown butter over the top.

Seared Scallops

Claire Mark, yogaview instructor

Seared scallops are elegant, easy, quick-cooking, and delicious. They are also a good source of vitamin B12, Omega-3 fatty acids, magnesium, and potassium. —Claire

Preparation time: 10 minutes
Total time: 10 minutes
Serves 2

6-8 jumbo scallops
1 tablespoon butter
salt to taste

Heat a cast iron pan on the stove. Rinse scallops, pat dry, and add salt. When pan is hot, add butter, and make sure pan is evenly coated.

Add scallops to pan and cook for 2-3 minutes on each side (they should be brown and seared).

Serve immediately.

Seared Salmon

Claire Mark, yogaview instructor

Salmon is my favorite fish to eat, and this recipe is so simple I make it all the time. Salmon is loaded with disease-fighting acids, minerals, and vitamins (omega 3s, vitamin D, vitamin B12, niacin, and selenium, just to name a few). It's also an excellent source of protein: one 4-ounce serving gives you almost 30 grams. —Claire

Preparation time: 15 minutes
Total time: 15 minutes
Serves 2

2 6-ounce pieces of salmon fillet, bones removed, skin on
2 teaspoons olive oil
1 teaspoon salt
black pepper to taste

Preheat oven to 375° degrees, and pre-heat cast iron pan on stove.

Rinse fish gently and pat dry.

With a spoon or brush, put one teaspoon of olive oil on each piece of fish, then add salt and black pepper (use about ½ a teaspoon of salt per piece of fish).

Place fish flesh side down on hot cast iron pan for 4 minutes, timed.

Flip fish (flesh should have brown crust) and then place salmon in the cast iron pan in the oven (just make sure you have oven mitts for your hands!) for 4 minutes, timed.

Remove from oven and serve!

Salmon En Croute

Claire Mark, yogaview instructor

This recipe originally comes from Quinn's mom--a family favorite. I changed a few things to make it a little healthier, but it still tastes fantastic! It's easy and fun to make too.
—Claire

Preparation time: 30 minutes
Total time: 45 minutes
Serves 4

4 6-oz. salmon filets, no skin
1 tablespoon minced garlic
2 tablespoons minced shallots
1 tablespoon minced chives

4 tablespoons cream cheese
1 package of puff pastry
1 egg
½ tablespoons (to grease baking sheet)

Preheat oven to 400° degrees. Wash and pat dry salmon.

Defrost pastry and cut into quarters. Lightly flour a cutting board and roll out pastry with a floured rolling pin until each piece of pastry is big enough to wrap like an envelope around the salmon. (You will need to re-flour the cutting board and rolling pin to avoid sticking.)

Place 1 piece of salmon in the middle of each piece of pastry, put 1 tablespoon of cream cheese on top of each piece of salmon, and gently spread it so it covers the length of the salmon. Combine garlic, shallots, and chives and place 1/4 of mixture on top of each section of cream cheese. Pull up the sides of the pastry and fold as you would an envelope, then press the edges down to seal. Brush tops with beaten egg.

Grease baking sheet with butter. Place salmon packages on baking sheet, and place in the oven until the top is golden brown (20-25 minutes). Remove from oven and serve immediately!

Whole Wheat Orzo Salad with Roasted Vegetables

Bridgett Cawley Piacenti, yogaview instructor

The roasted vegetables in this recipe give the salad a rich, deep flavor, and the feta and pine nuts add a perfect salty crunch. —Bridgett

Preparation time: 30 minutes
Total time: 50 minutes
Serves 6

1 medium-sized eggplant, peeled and diced
1 each of red, yellow, and orange bell peppers, diced
1 small red onion, diced
2 garlic cloves, minced
1/3 cup olive oil (I typically start with ¼ cup and work up a bit)
1½ teaspoon salt
½ teaspoon black pepper
½ lb. whole wheat orzo or regular orzo

For the dressing:
1/3 cup freshly squeezed lemon juice (juice of 2-3 lemons)
1/3 cup olive oil (I use a little less, about ¼ cup and then add if needed)
1 teaspoon salt
½ teaspoon black pepper
4 scallions, minced
¼ cup pine nuts, toasted
¾ cup feta or goat cheese, diced
15 fresh basil leaves, julienned
1/3 cup currants

Preheat oven to 425°.

Toss eggplant, peppers, onion, and garlic with olive oil, salt, and pepper. On baking sheet, roast 30 minutes or until browned. Turn vegetables one time while roasting.

Cook orzo in salted water, 7-9 minutes. Transfer to serving bowl.

Add cooked veggies to orzo and add dressing. Make sure all liquid from baking sheet mixes in with orzo. Add dressing, scallions, cheese, nuts, basil, and currants before serving.

Enjoy!

Quinoa and Legume Salad

Susan Kearney Mathews, friend of yogaview

I especially enjoy quinoa because it always reminds me of my son Quinn. Quinoa is a good choice for vegetarians because it is a complete protein supplying nine amino acids, and it tastes good too! Cut ingredients in half to make a smaller amount or save leftovers for the next day. —Susan

Preparation time: 40 minutes
Serves 10-12

16 oz. red quinoa
4 cups vegetable stock
1 15 oz. can black beans, drained and rinsed
1 15 oz. can kidney beans, drained, **not** rinsed
Corn Salsa (see recipe page 52)

1 seedless cucumber, peeled in strips and diced
3 avocados, diced
juice of 2 limes
2 tablespoons olive oil
salt to taste

Rinse quinoa thoroughly (do not skip this step). Wash quinoa several times in cold water. Bring 4 cups of veggie stock to boil. Add rinsed quinoa to veggie stock, cover, reduce heat and simmer for 15 minutes or until stock is absorbed. After quinoa is cooked, let stand for 5 minutes to cool before adding black beans, kidney beans, corn salad, and cucumber.

Add lime juice, olive oil, and salt to taste. Garnish with diced avocados and cilantro leaves. Enjoy!

Fancy Macaroni and Cheese

Claire Mark, yogaview instructor

This version of mac and cheese will remind you of your childhood, but with a grown-up twist! —Claire

Preparation time: 30 minutes
Total time: 60 minutes
Serves 4-6

2 heads broccoli
½ tablespoon olive oil
½ pound Cavatappi pasta
1 cup shredded smoked Gouda
1 cup shredded sharp cheddar

3 tablespoons butter
3 tablespoons flour
3 cups whole milk
1 cup fresh bread crumbs (sourdough if possible, but any day-old bread will do)

Preheat the oven to 375°.

Fill a pot of water on the stove and bring to a boil. Add a pinch of salt. Place one piece of torn-up day-old bread in a food processor and pulse until reduced to crumbs.

Heat the olive oil in a skillet. While the oil is warming, cut the florets off the broccoli into small bite-sized pieces. When the oil is hot, add broccoli and toss until lightly coated with the oil. Cook for about 8-10 minutes or until the broccoli is brown on the edges. Remove from heat and set aside.

When the water has boiled, add the pasta and cook for half the amount of time suggested on the box. When cooking time is done, drain pasta and set aside.

While the water is boiling, heat the butter and flour in a separate pot, and whisk the two together. Add the milk to the butter and flour and turn the heat down very low. Whisk the milk in and then slowly add the Gouda cheese, continuing to whisk, then add the cheddar cheese, continuing to whisk until mixture is creamy and smooth. Add a teaspoon of salt and a dash of pepper.

Place the pasta and broccoli in a baking dish. Add the cheese sauce and mix it around until it coats all the pasta and broccoli. Place the bread crumbs on top and put it in the oven for 30 minutes or until bread crumbs are brown on top.

Remove from oven, and add a pinch of truffle salt to individual bowls of pasta. Serve hot.

Portobello Mushroom Burgers

Claire Mark, yogaview Instructor

This recipe is a great meat-free way to make a burger. Portobello mushrooms are full of nutrients (including antioxidants) and amazingly rich in flavor--this recipe is easy to make and so good even your burger-loving friends will enjoy it! I've listed my favorite burger toppings below, but you can get creative and experiment with using whatever condiments you like on a regular burger. —Claire

Preparation time: 20 minutes
Total time: 45-55 minutes
Serves 4

4 large Portobello mushroom caps
2 garlic cloves, minced
¼ cup olive oil
2 large white or yellow onions

4 burger buns (to make gluten-free, omit
    or use gluten-free buns)
a handful of fresh arugula
good blue cheese (to taste)
salt and black pepper

Preheat the oven to 400°.

De-stem and clean mushrooms, then put them in a large ziplock plastic bag with the garlic, half of the olive oil, salt, and pepper. Mix all the ingredients around in the bag and then set aside to marinate.

Put a pan over medium heat; once the pan is heated, add half of the remaining olive oil. Cut the onions into thin slices and add to the pan when hot. It will take some time to cook them down and caramelize them (35-45 minutes); stir occasionally and add the remaining olive oil when the pan seems to be drying.

While the onions are cooking, place the marinated mushrooms on a cooking sheet, smooth side up, and set in the oven to bake. This will take about 20 minutes; they're done when the mushrooms look a little wilted around the edges.

When the mushrooms and onions are almost done cooking, toast the burger buns in the toaster or in the oven on a separate baking sheet.

To assemble the burgers, spread some blue cheese on the bottom bun, then add the caramelized onions, Portobello mushroom and ¼ of the arugula. Serve while warm!

Gourmet Grilled Cheese

Vivian Roumboulas, yogaview student

This upscale grilled cheese goes great with Carrot Fries (see recipe page 62)! —Vivian

Preparation time: 45-60 minutes
Total time: 45-60 minutes
Serves 4

For the sandwiches:
1 loaf rustic pumpernickel or rye bread
1-2 tablespoons unsalted butter, softened
1 cup Emmentaler or other firm Swiss cheese
1 cup sharp cheddar cheese, grated

For the caramelized onions:
2 white or sweet onions, sliced thinly
1-2 tablespoons olive oil
Garnish: cornichons and Creole mustard

Heat sauté pan over medium-high heat. Add olive oil, then add onions in as thin a layer as possible. Once onions start to become translucent, reduce heat to medium. Leave onions alone. They will start to shrink and the bottom of the pan will develop a deep, caramel-like color. Stir, only occasionally, until onions are soft and a somewhat uniform amber-caramel color (about 35-45 minutes). Remove from heat.

Slice bread in ½- ¾ inch slices from center of loaf of bread, enough for four sandwiches. Butter one side of each of the slices of bread (this will allow you to control the amount of butter in the pan and on the sandwiches).

In large sauté pan or griddle, place half of the bread butter side down on medium-high heat. Cover each slice with equal amounts of both cheeses and top with caramelized onions. Add enough cheese to cover onions. Top with other half of bread, this time butter side up, and use a spatula to press bread down lightly. After about 2-3 minutes flip sandwiches carefully. After 2-3 minutes, turn heat down to medium and cover pan with lid. Remove lid after about 2 minutes and check to see how melted the cheese looks. Continue just until thoroughly melted and bread has a golden brown color.

Move sandwiches to plates, cut in half, and serve with cornichons and Creole mustard for dipping.

Choose Your Own Adventure Pesto

Anna Argeropoulos, yogaview instructor

Pesto is my favorite thing to make from the bounty of my little backyard garden, and I've enjoyed experimenting with different pestos. You can vary from the traditional basil/ pine nut combination by taking a leafy green, adding nuts of your choice, some oil, some garlic, perhaps some cheese, and grinding it all up in your food processor. Enjoy experimenting with different combinations and flavors! —Anna

Preparation time: 20 minutes
Total time: 20 minutes

2 cups greens *(choose one from below)*
   basil
   chive *(works well with mint!)*
   kale
   arugula
   nasturtium leaves
   spinach
   Swiss chard
   beet greens
   tarragon
   sage
   green beans

¼ cup nuts/seeds *(choose one from below)*
   pine nuts
   walnuts
   pistachios
   cashews
   almonds
   pecans
   sesame seeds

3 medium garlic cloves, minced
½ cup Parmigiano-Reggiano cheese
   (optional—leave out to make vegan)
½ cup olive oil
sea salt and pepper to taste

Combine the greens with the nuts and pulse several times in a food processor. Add the garlic and pulse a few more times. Slowly add the olive oil in a stream, pausing to scrape down the sides of the processor with a spatula as needed. Add the cheese (if using) and pulse until blended. Add salt and pepper to taste.

Pesto's uses are endless! Try it stirred into a quiche filling, mixed with scrambled eggs, stirred into pasta or rice salad, as a replacement for tomato sauce on pizza, mixed with yogurt to create vegetable dip, added to sauces and dressings, mixed into mayonnaise, or just spread on toasted bread!

Pesto is delicious served fresh, but will keep for 3 to 4 days in the refrigerator (be sure to top it with olive oil before you refrigerate, which will help it keep longer). Frozen pesto retains great flavor and will keep for up to a year.

Homemade Tomato Sauce

Carole Mark, friend of yogaview

It's easy to buy a jar of tomato sauce, but nothing tastes better then homemade sauce, especially when the tomatoes are fresh and in season. Tomatoes contain lycopene, a vital antioxidant that helps fight against cancerous cells, and the aroma of the garlic and tomatoes cooking together will make your kitchen smell fantastic! This sauce can be made in advance, frozen, or used immediately. —Carole

Preparation time: 20 minutes
Total time: 80 minutes
Serves 6-8

12 to 15 medium-sized fresh plum
   tomatoes
½ cup fresh basil, chopped
½ to 1 whole head garlic, chopped
   (depending on how much you like garlic!)

3 tablespoons olive oil
2-3 tablespoons of tomato paste
optional: ¼ teaspoon hot pepper flakes

Blanch tomatoes for 1 minute in boiling water. Remove, let cool, and peel. Drain, then chop and set aside. (Alternative: use boxed or canned plum tomatoes.)

In a large skillet, sauté garlic in olive oil. When garlic is translucent, add basil and sauté for several minutes. If using, add hot pepper flakes and sauté for another minute.

Add tomatoes and simmer for an hour or more uncovered. If you want thicker sauce, add tomato paste.

Use with pasta, fresh vegetables, breakfast eggs, or spread on toasted bread with your favorite cheese.

Garbanzo Beans with Spiced Squash

Jessica Quinn, wife of Tom Quinn, co-founder of yogaview

Ghee is clarified butter frequently used in Indian cuisine. This recipe is great served over jasmine rice. As you add the spices, keep in mind there are three teaspoons to one tablespoon. —Jessica

Preparation time: 35 minutes
Total time: 1 hour, 20 minutes
Serves 4-6

4 cups garbanzo beans
1 butternut squash, cored, skinned, and
   cut into ½ inch cubes
6 cups tomato sauce
1 1/2 cups sweet onions, chopped finely
6 garlic gloves, minced
1 cup cashews
3 tablespoons fresh ginger, grated
2 tablespoon turmeric

1 tablespoon paprika
3 teaspoons cinnamon
1 teaspoon cayenne (or less,
   to taste)
1 tablespoon ghee
1 cup cilantro
optional: 2 tablespoons brown sugar

For the garnish: lime, cilantro, and goat cheese

Melt the ghee in a pot over medium heat. Add garlic and onion and cook until translucent. Add the squash and 3 cups of tomato sauce to the pot, then add 2 teaspoons of cinnamon and ginger and half a teaspoon of the turmeric and paprika, sprinkling evenly. Simmer mixture for 20 minutes.

When the squash starts to soften, add the rest of the ingredients (including brown sugar if using) and stir. Cook for another 40 minutes. If the mixture starts to get dry, add more tomato sauce.

When done, pour spiced squash mixture over jasmine rice in bowls. Garnish with cilantro and goat cheese and fresh lime juice. Serve with some fresh garlic naan or good crusty bread.

Vegetable Lasagna

Claire Mark, yogaview instructor

Feel free to use different vegetables in this dish–eggplant, yellow squash, or red pepper would all be good as well! —Claire

Preparation time: 30 to 45 minutes (depends on how fast you chop)
Total time: 90 minutes
Serves 8

1 bag (5 oz.) baby spinach
1 yellow onion, finely chopped
4 cloves garlic, finely chopped
1 medium zucchini, finely chopped
2 carrots, finely chopped
1 16-ounce container white button
    mushrooms, finely chopped
10 large basil leaves, finely chopped
½ cup good white wine

1 can whole plum tomatoes
1 box lasagna noodles
1 15 oz. container ricotta
1 cup grated Parmesan cheese
2 eggs
2 balls fresh mozzarella, sliced into
    thin pieces
2 tablespoons olive oil
salt and pepper to taste

Preheat oven to 350° degrees. Put a pot on to boil the pasta, and put a smaller pot on to cook the spinach. While the water is coming to a boil, chop up all the vegetables and set them aside. Heat a large skillet and add the olive oil. When the oil is warm, add the onions and garlic. Cook for a minute or two until the onions are translucent. Then add the zucchini and carrots, and cook for another few minutes until they are soft. Add the mushrooms and continue to cook--when the mushrooms are soft, add the white wine, salt, and pepper. Cook some of the wine down, then add the tomatoes (crushing them with your hands before putting them in the sauce) and the basil. Cook the sauce until most of the liquid is boiled out, so that the sauce isn't too soupy.

At the same time, cook the spinach for just one minute in boiling water. Take it out and run it under cold water to stop the cooking, squeeze out all the liquid, and finely chop it. Mix the spinach, ricotta, ½ cup of the Parmesan cheese, and the two eggs and set aside. Cook the pasta al dente and set aside.

When the sauce has cooked down, you are ready to layer the lasagna! In a baking dish, put a thin layer of the sauce, followed by a layer pasta, then the ricotta mixture, a few slices of the mozzarella, and 1/3 the total amount of sauce. Repeat two more times; pasta, ricotta mixture, mozzarella, sauce. At the end, sprinkle the rest of the Parmesan cheese on top.

Cook with tin foil on top for 20 minutes, then take tin foil off and cook for another 20 minutes. Take out and let cool for 10 minutes before serving.

Shrimp and Pea Risotto with Basil and Mint

Michael Flockhart, yogaview instructor

The key to great risotto is to keep stirring and to add small amounts of liquid at a time. Fresh peas are readily available in the spring, and can really add to the overall flavor of the dish. To make this dish vegetarian, simply leave out the shrimp. —Michael

Preparation time: 25 minutes
Total time: 50-60 minutes
Serves 6

For the pea mash:
½ cup fresh or frozen peas, shelled
1-2 tablespoons butter
¼–½ cup vegetable stock

To make the pea mash, fry ½ a cup of peas, butter, and vegetable stock. Cook until tender, mash, and set aside to add to risotto later.

For the risotto:
1 tablespoon olive oil
3 shallots or 1 medium onion, finely chopped
2 cloves garlic, finely chopped
2 celery stalks, finely chopped
14 oz. Arborio rice
1¼ cup vermouth or dry white wine
5 cups fish or vegetable stock

5 tablespoons butter
1 lb. raw shrimp, uncooked, shelled (optional)
½ cup fresh or frozen peas, shelled
½ cup fresh basil, chopped
¼ cup fresh mint, chopped
juice of 1 lemon
sea salt and freshly ground pepper to taste
drizzle of olive oil (once plated)

Heat stock in a pot. In a separate pot, heat the olive oil, add the garlic, celery, and shallots or onions, then fry slowly for about 4 minutes. When the vegetables have softened, add the rice and turn up the heat.

The rice will now begin to fry so keep stirring it. After a minute it will look slightly translucent. Add the vermouth or wine and keep stirring. Let the alcohol evaporate.

cont'd.

Once the vermouth or wine has cooked into the rice, add your first ladle of hot stock and a good pinch of salt. Turn down the heat to a high simmer so the rice doesn't cook too quickly on the outside. Keep adding ladlefuls of stock, stirring, allowing each ladleful to be absorbed before adding the next. This process will take about 15 minutes. Rice should be soft but still have a bite. Season carefully with salt and pepper.

Add pea mash, plus the shrimp and the rest of the peas and simmer for 2 minutes–shrimp and peas take no time to cook.

Add fresh herbs and squeeze in the lemon juice. Remove from heat and add butter. Stir, place a lid on the pan, and allow it to sit for 2-3 minutes. Plate and drizzle individual plates with olive oil. Enjoy!

Curry Eggplant Masala Terrine

Valerie Bolon, yogaview student

This recipe is a multi-step dish that takes some extra time to prepare, but is well worth the efforts. (Also, the curry can be made ahead of time and refrigerated or frozen.) The steps are as follow: first make the curry paste, then prepare the eggplant, next sauté the eggplant, then assemble the terrine, then bake. —Valerie

Recipe for curry:

1 carrot, peeled and diced	3-5 cloves garlic, chopped
1 onion, diced	1 teaspoon ground cumin
2 stalks celery, diced	1 teaspoon ground coriander
5 tomatoes, cored and rough chopped	½ teaspoon cinnamon
1 tablespoon tomato paste	2 cups vegetable stock or water
1 stalk lemongrass, cut into small pieces	2 tablespoons fish sauce

Place a medium-sized saucepot over medium heat and add cooking oil. Add onion and sauté 2-3 minutes (until translucent). Then add carrot, celery, tomato, garlic, lemongrass, and tomato paste and continue to sauté another 3-5 minutes until vegetables begin to soften. Add cumin, coriander, and cinnamon and cook another 3-5 minutes, stirring frequently. Add stock and fish sauce and let cook about 20 more minutes (until the vegetables are very soft and the mixture becomes thick). Remove from heat and puree in a blender or food processor until the curry is smooth. Remove and set aside.

This mixture can be made ahead of time and stored in either the refrigerator or freezer.

Recipe for eggplant:

2-3 large eggplants, cut into slices 1/2 inch thick
kosher salt (do not substitute non-kosher salt, as it will not absorb moisture as well)

Slice the eggplant in 1/2 inch thick slices, keeping the slices as consistent as possible. Place a flat layer of sliced eggplant in a large baking dish, then sprinkle the eggplant with a generous amount of salt. (This salting process is to remove the moisture that naturally occurs in the eggplant. The salt will be washed off later.) Continue to stack each piece of eggplant on top of the previous layer, and keep salting each layer until all the eggplant is stacked and salted in the baking dish. Let it sit for about an hour so the moisture can rise up to the surface. Then remove the eggplant and rinse each piece in the sink with water (rinse thoroughly to avoid oversalting the final dish!). Once rinsed, lay the eggplant flat on a baking tray. Pat dry with paper towels. Dry thoroughly and set aside.

Sautéing the eggplant:

2 cups flour
1 tablespoon yellow curry powder
1 tablespoon hot curry powder
1 teaspoon sea or kosher salt

vegetable oil or other cooking oil
   (which you will keep adding to sauté
   pan periodically)
1 cup Parmesan cheese, goat cheese,
   or other cheese of your choice

To prepare the eggplant for cooking, put the flour in a dish or bowl. Add both curry powders and salt to the flour and mix with your hands. Place a large sauté pan over medium heat. Add cooking oil, enough to cover the bottom of the pan. Take a slice of eggplant and dredge it in the flour mixture on both sides, then shake off the excess. Place in the hot sauté pan and let sit for about 2-3 minutes on each side. Remove from heat and place on a baking sheet to cool. Continue to sauté each piece of eggplant (this can be done a few pieces at a time). Continue to add more oil to the sauté pan as the eggplant will soak it up while cooking.

Assembling the terrine:

Preheat oven to 375°. Grease a baking dish. Place the cooked eggplant in a layer in the bottom of the baking dish--pack it tightly and press it firmly to the bottom. There should be no holes through to the bottom of the dish. Take several spoonfuls of the curry and spread it across the eggplant layer, then sprinkle some cheese on top of the layer. Once again, add another layer of eggplant, press firmly into the baking dish. Add a layer of curry, then cheese. Continue this process until all the eggplant is used up and the baking dish is filled. Sprinkle the top with cheese and then place in the oven and bake until golden brown and the top layer of cheese is melted (about 15 minutes). Remove, cut, and serve.

This dish can be made ahead of time. Simply cool completely and cover and store in the refrigerator until ready to serve.

attention to detail

Paying attention to the small things, whether it's rooting down with your little toe in cobra pose, or adding that last flavorful or decorative garnish to a dish, keeps both the yoga practice and the experience of cooking fun, exciting, and ever-evolving.

attention to detail

desserts, breads & snacks

Cardamom Fruit Salad

Brooks Hall, yogaview instructor

This recipe takes fruit salad to a new level—the scent of the cardamom and cilantro is amazing, and the spices enhance the taste of the fruit without overwhelming it. You can experiment with different fruits as well--I added pineapple because I had one on hand, and it tasted great. —Jennifer

Preparation time: 20 minutes
Total time: 1 hour, 20 minutes
Serves 4

1½ cups red flesh of papaya (1 large papaya), cubed
⅛ cup black seeds from the papaya
1 cup banana, sliced
1 cup strawberries, sliced
1 cup blueberries

½ cup dried unsweetened coconut
⅛ cup dried currants
1 teaspoon ground cardamom
¼ cup chopped cilantro
juice of ½ a lemon

Place all the fruit except the banana in a large bowl. Squeeze lemon over the fruit in the bowl and add cardamom. Toss gently with a large spoon to evenly distribute the lemon juice, coconut, and spice.

Sprinkle the top with cilantro.

Cover and chill for an hour (or more). Add the banana and toss one more time right before serving.

Maya Tulum Granola

Chef Mitch Toloza Jimenez, friend of yogaview

Maya Tulum is a place dear to many yogaview students—it's a gorgeous yoga & wellness spa in Mexico where Claire and Quinn lead a retreat every winter. In addition to yoga, the beach, and the ocean, Maya Tulum offers fantastic fresh food, and their granola is out of this world. —Jennifer

Preparation time: 1 hour
Total time: 1 day
Makes approximately 1.5 lbs. of granola

6½ cups old-fashioned oats
1 ½ cups raw pecan halves
1 cup raw whole almonds

1 ¼ cup raisins
½ cup amaranth
1 cup honey

Preheat oven to 400°. Combine oatmeal and ½ cup honey, mix well, and place on baking sheet. Bake in oven for approximately 45 minutes, stirring every 10 minutes or so until it turns a nutty brown and smells nutty. Set aside to cool.

Reduce oven temperature to 375°.

Place nuts on baking sheet (separated, the pecans will toast more quickly) and toast in oven, watching carefully so they don't burn.

Remove before they become too dark, and pour remaining honey over. Stir until nuts are well-coated and put back in the oven until well combined.

Remove and transfer nuts to an oiled container to cool.

After oats and nuts have cooled completely, mix together in an airtight container and let sit without opening for 24 hours.

The following day, add raisins and amaranth.

Granola will stay fresh in a closed ziplock bag or container at room temperature for 15-30 days and 1-2 months if refrigerated.

Decadent Date Bars

Dorie Silverman, yogaview instructor

Dates are a great source of fiber and contain high levels of potassium, magnesium, copper, and manganese. Dorie's date bars are not only healthy , they're infamously addictive--I never enter her house without checking the fridge to see if she might have made a pan recently. They're that good. —Jennifer

Preparation time: 10 minutes
Total time: 10 minutes
Makes 9-12 bars

4 cups of pecans and almonds (I like to do half and half)
22 Medjool dates, pitted (about 2 cups room temperature, not refrigerated)
2 tablespoons raw cocoa powder

1 tablespoon cinnamon
other optional ingredients: goji berries, maca powder, banana chips, raisins, dark chocolate

Combine nuts and dates in a food processor. You will need to stop at least 5-6 times scrape the sides and help the mixture to combine. During that process, add your spices.

Once the natural oils of the nuts come out in the dates and start to bind everything together, the consistency of your mixture will be a bit sticky. Check it with your fingers. Once it's all bound together, transfer to a 9 x 9-inch pan with a lid. Press it flat with a spatula and decorate the top with pecans.

Cut into rectangles, wrap, and either serve or refrigerate.

Fanouropita Greek Prayer Cake

Vivian Roumboulas, yogaview student

I was researching Greek desserts and stumbled upon the folklore for this one. Generally it's made with a prayer or wish in mind. The condition is that the cake must be given away after you make it, and you keep making cakes until the prayer/wish is answered. It's vegan and super moist—delicious even without making a wish. —Vivian

Preparation time: 15 minutes
Total time: 3 hours
Makes one 9 x 13-inch pan

4 cups flour
4 teaspoon baking powder
1½ teaspoon cinnamon
¼ teaspoon allspice
¼ teaspoon pumpkin pie spice or
   ⅛ teaspoon ground cloves
½ teaspoon salt
½ cup safflower or other light oil
½ cup olive oil
1 cup plus 2 tablespoons sugar
zest of 1 large navel orange

2 cups fresh squeezed orange juice
   with pulp
¼ cup orange liqueur (such as Grand
   Marnier) plus 2 tablespoons
¼ cup brandy (such as Metaxa) plus
   2 tablespoons
¾ cup golden raisins
⅓ cup currants
1 cup walnuts, toasted and roughly
   chopped
powdered sugar for garnish

Preheat oven to 350°. Take dried fruit and put in small saucepan with 2 tablespoons each of orange liqueur and brandy. Heat until just warm, turn off heat, then cover and set aside. Grease and flour 9 x 13 x 2-inch Pyrex dish.

In large bowl, combine flour with baking powder, spices, and salt until thoroughly combined, set aside. In mixing bowl fitted with paddle attachment, mix oil, sugar, orange juice, zest, and the remaining brandy and liqueur, and mix until sugar begins to dissolve (about 3 minutes).

Drain raisins and currants. Add them, along with flour mixture, to wet ingredients and mix just until no traces of flour remain.

Pour evenly into greased dish and bake 45 minutes to one hour, until toothpick inserted in center of cake comes out clean.

Allow to cool in pan on wire rack at least two hours.

Dust with powdered sugar.

Semolina Extra Virgin Olive Oil Cake

Erik Hecimovich, yogaview student

This cake reminds me of the sweets that I enjoyed with my Greek family growing up. It's not super sweet, but more like a cross between a bread and a cake, suitable for a snack in the afternoon with tea or coffee, or as a simple dessert, dusted with a little powdered sugar, fresh mint, and a simple sorbet or ice cream after dinner. —Vivian

Preparation time: 15 minutes, plus 1 hour for batter to rest
Total time: 1 hour, 15 minutes
Makes one 8-inch cake/12 average-sized pieces, or 8 large pieces

¾ cup pastry flour (if white pastry flour is unavailable, use ½ cup unbleached all-purpose and ¼ cup cake flour)
½ cup semolina flour
¾ cup sugar
½ teaspoon ground ginger
¼ teaspoon salt

½ teaspoon baking powder
2 egg yolks
½ cup buttermilk
¼ cup extra virgin olive oil
zest from 2 lemons
2 and ¼ teaspoon orange flower water (available at Middle Eastern markets)

Preheat oven to 350°.

Grease and lightly flour an 8-inch round cake pan. Measure all dry ingredients into one bowl. Stir with a whisk to combine thoroughly. Measure all wet ingredients into another bowl. Stir gently.

In a clean mixing bowl, alternate mixing these two bowls of ingredients together, starting with wet and ending with dry, combining just until mixed. Do not overstir.
Let batter rest for one hour.

Pour batter evenly into cake pan, tapping gently to remove any air bubbles.

Bake for 45 minutes to an hour, checking for done-ness after 35 minutes (insert a toothpick, if it's done, it should come out clean).

Allow to cool in pan on cooling rack for at least an hour before serving. This cake looks lovely dusted with powdered sugar.

Grilled Peaches with Ricotta and Balsamic Glaze

Carolyn Rosenberg, yogaview student

If you don't have fresh peaches on hand, you can substitute nectarines or even apricots in this recipe. —Carolyn

Preparation time: 20 minutes
Total time: 20 minutes
Serves 4-8

4 ripe peaches (can be slightly firm),
   halved
¾ cup fresh ricotta cheese
¼ cup olive oil for rubbing on grill and
   peach halves
mint or tarragon sprigs for garnish

For the balsamic glaze:
2 tablespoons balsamic vinegar

Clean grill, lightly oil and put heat on medium-high. Brush olive oil on peaches. Grill 4-5 minutes a side or until there is a nice char. Let stand for 5-10 minutes (the grilling can be done several hours in advance).

To make the balsamic glaze, put balsamic vinegar in a small saucepan over low heat, and cook it until it "reduces" (i.e., much of the liquid evaporates) by half.

When ready to serve, place 1-2 tablespoons of the ricotta in the center of each peach half and drizzle with balsamic glaze. Add mint or tarragon sprigs for garnish.

Maple Syrup Kettle Corn

Jennifer Boeder, yogaview instructor

This snack is sweet, savory, and crunchy, and the coconut oil not only adds amazing flavor but has many health benefits (it's great for your bones and your digestive system). High-quality maple syrup and fancy salt makes it even more gourmet. —Jennifer

Preparation time: 10 minutes
Total time: 10 minutes
Serves 2

½ cup popcorn kernels
3 tablespoons coconut oil

¼ cup high-grade maple syrup
sea salt to taste

Heat oil over medium heat in a heavy-bottomed pot (one with a glass lid is really helpful). Make sure oil covers the bottom of the pot, then add kernels and spread them evenly. Cover and let it pop; depending on heaviness of your cookware, you may need to shake the pot continuously during popping to keep heat even and ensure the kernels don't burn. Once the popping slows down, remove from heat (taking it off just before it's all popped also helps prevent burning). Pour popcorn into a large bowl and drizzle maple syrup over it as you stir (do this step while popcorn is still warm so that the syrup sticks). Add salt to taste, stir, and serve.

Parmesan Truffled Popcorn

Claire Mark, yogaview instructor

Preparation time: 10 minutes
Total time: 10 minutes
Serves 2

½ cup popcorn kernels
3 tablespoons olive oil

¼ cup Parmesan cheese, grated
truffle salt to taste

Heat a 2.5 quart pot on the stove until hot. Add olive oil (enough to cover the bottom of the pot). When oil is hot, add corn kernels to cover the bottom of the pot in a single layer. Cover pot and let sit until you hear the first corn kernel pop, then lift and shake over heat continuously until popping stops (about 2-3 minutes). Immediately take popcorn and pour it into a bowl—add the rest of the above ingredients and serve.

Cranberry Oatmeal Cookies

Patti Lupo, yogaview instructor

The oats in these cookies are a great source of iron and fiber, and add a heart-healthy element to your dessert. —Patti

Preparation time: 30 minutes
Total time: 45 minutes
Makes 24 cookies

⅓ cup flour
1½ cups old-fashioned rolled oats
1 teaspoon baking soda
½ teaspoon salt
6 tablespoons unsalted butter
¾ cup packed brown sugar

1 cup dried cranberries
1 teaspoon vanilla extract
1 large egg (lightly beaten)
3 oz. bittersweet chocolate chips
cooking spray

Preheat oven to 350°. Combine flour, oats, baking soda, and salt in large bowl. Stir with a whisk.

Melt butter in small saucepan over low heat. Remove from heat. Add brown sugar, stirring until smooth. Add sugar mixture to flour mixture. Beat with a mixer at medium speed until well blended. Add vanilla, egg, and cranberries. Beat until combined.

Fold in chocolate chips. Drop dough by tablespoons on baking sheets coated with cooking spray. Bake at 350° for 12 minutes. Cool on sheets 3 minutes. Remove from sheets to wire racks. Cool and serve.

Honey Chocolate Chip Cookies

Erik Hecimovich, yogaview student

Using high-grade, strongly flavored honey adds subtle but distinctive aroma and taste to these cookies, and adds a fresh twist to a common recipe. There are more than 300 distinct varieties of honey produced in the U.S. alone, so experiment away! —*Erik*

Preparation time: 30 minutes
Total time: 45 minutes
Makes about 3 dozen cookies

9 oz. butter, room temperature
1½ cups white sugar (10 oz.)
¾ cup very lightly packed light brown sugar (4.5 oz.)
1-2 large eggs (2 oz.)
1 tablespoon yogurt (½ oz.)
1 tablespoon (½ oz.) strongly flavored honey (wildflower and litchi honey work well)

3 cups unbleached all-purpose flour, spooned and leveled (13 oz.)
¾ cups or bread flour, spooned and leveled (5 oz.)
2½ teaspoons baking soda (4.5 g)
1¾ teaspoons salt (5 g)
6 oz. dark chocolate chunks/chips
6 oz. milk chocolate chunks/chips

Preheat oven to 350°. In a bowl, combine flours, baking soda, and salt. Stir with a whisk until combined and set aside.

In mixing bowl, cream butter and sugars with paddle attachment until light and fluffy, about 3 to 5 minutes.

Gradually add eggs until combined, scrape down sides of the bowl. Slowly add dry ingredients on **low** speed until just combined **(do not overmix)**. Gently fold in chocolate chips.

Using tablespoons or your hands, roll dough into balls and place on cookie sheet. Bake for 12-14 minutes or until light golden brown. These cookies are slightly lighter than traditional chocolate chip cookies in color, so be careful not to overbake.

Cool before serving.

Sweet and Savory Banana Bread

Molly Boeder Harris, yogaview instructor

I have always loved the homemade breads my mom baked and still makes for our family. I have a particular affinity for the sweet and savory combination in her banana bread, and have experimented for years with creating my own take on a relatively common treat. You can be creative with special touches like applesauce, honey, chocolate chips, and nuts--find a balance of flavor that you like best! —Molly

Preparation time: 25 minutes
Total time: 1 hour, 20 minutes
Makes 2 loaves (about 8 slices per loaf)

Dry ingredients:
2 cups whole wheat flour
1¾ cups sugar
1 tablespoon baking powder
½ teaspoon baking soda
1 teaspoon salt
1 tablespoon cinnamon
1 cup walnuts, chopped

Wet ingredients:
3 very ripe bananas, mashed
2 eggs
½ cup butter, melted
¼ cup sour milk (add a dash of apple cider vinegar to milk to sour)
1 teaspoon vanilla
⅓ cup applesauce
1 tablespoon honey
1 cup chocolate chips (optional)

Preheat oven to 350°.

Mix dry ingredients together in a large bowl and set aside. Mash bananas in a separate bowl, then add the remaining wet ingredients and mix together. Pour wet ingredients into large bowl of dry ingredients and (if adding) slowly fold in chocolate chips.

Stir until mostly smooth. Grease 2 bread pans and pour mixture into pans. Bake 45-55 minutes (until loaves are beginning to brown). Remove from oven and cool 30 minutes before serving.

Crispy Cocoa Cookies

Erik Hecimovich, yogaview student

The toasting of the nuts and the chilling of the dough takes some extra time, but these cookies are so unusual and so pretty that they're well worth the effort.
—Vivian

Preparation time: 45 minutes, plus 1 hour to chill dough
Total time: 1 hour 45 minutes
Makes about 3 dozen cookies

8.5 oz. butter, room temperature (240.5 grams)
2 cups plus 2 tablespoons powdered sugar (262.5 grams)
2 eggs
1½ cups hazelnuts, skinned (192.5 grams)

¾ cup pistachios (96 grams)
1¾ cup flour (192.5 grams)
¾ cup cocoa powder (48 grams)
½ teaspoon salt (2.5 g)
1 teaspoon cinnamon

Preheat oven to 350°. Toast nuts in oven for approximately 7 minutes or until lightly golden brown, making sure they do not burn. Let cool. Place nuts in food processor and grind until crumbly but not dust.

Sift the flour cinnamon and cocoa powder together. Cream the butter and sugar with paddle attachment for 3-5 minutes or until light and fluffy.

Gradually add egg to combine, scraping the bowl as necessary. Add flour mixture and mix just to combine. Gently fold in nuts. Roll dough into logs, chill for 1 hour, then cut into desired thickness (1/8-1/4 inch).

Bake for 10-14 minutes until done, depending on size. Allow to cool completely before storing in airtight container.

Lemon Ricotta Cheesecake

Erik Hecimovich, yogaview student

I've always loved cheesecake and this version blew my mind. Its texture is much lighter than most American cheesecakes, and the freshness of the lemon zest is wonderful.
—Claire

Preparation time: 30 minutes
Total time: 90 minutes
Makes 9-inch cheesecake

For the crust:
1 ½ cups finely ground graham crackers or chocolate wafers
5 teaspoons melted butter
⅓ cup sugar
⅛ teaspoon salt

For the filling:
1 lb. whole milk ricotta
8 oz. cream cheese
1 cup sugar
¼ teaspoon salt
zest from 2 lemons
4 eggs, plus 2 egg yolks
1 cup crème fraîche

Preheat oven to 350°. Invert the bottom of a 9-9.5 inch springform pan (to allow for easier removal). Attach the sides and butter the pan.

Mix all crust ingredients together, press into the bottom and one inch up the sides of the pan. Refrigerate for at least an hour.

In a food processor, mix ricotta, cream cheese, sugar, salt, lemon zest, eggs, and yolks until smooth.

Pour mixture into mixing bowl and gently fold in the crème fraîche with a spatula. Remove crust from refrigerator and wrap the exterior in heavy-duty foil. Place foil-wrapped pan into a large baking/roasting pan and pour hot water into roasting pan to come slightly higher than halfway up the sides of springform pan.

Gently pour cheesecake filling into springform pan and place pan/water bath into the preheated oven. Bake 45 minutes to 1 hour, or slightly longer until filling is just set.

Cool completely and run knife along the sides of the pan to release cake.

Zucchini Bread

Nicole Thompson, yogaview instructor

Making this bread when zucchini is in season will result in the best flavor. Serve it garnished with chocolate chips for a fantastic dessert option. —Nicole

Preparation time: 10 minutes
Total time: 90 minutes
Makes 1 loaf pan

2 eggs, beaten
½ cup safflower oil
¾ cup sugar
1 teaspoon vanilla
1 cup shredded zucchini
1½ cup whole wheat pastry or
   non-bleached white flour

½ teaspoon baking soda
¼ teaspoon baking powder
¾ teaspoon salt
2 teaspoon cinnamon
2 teaspoon coconut oil (or enough to line
   two 9 x 5-inch loaf pans)

Add all dry ingredients to wet. Stir, but don't overmix. Pour batter in oiled loaf pan. Bake at 350° degrees for approximately 1 hour—test for doneness by inserting a toothpick (when it comes out clean, the bread is done). Cool for 20 minutes, then let rest on cooling rack before serving.

Cranberry Cornbread with Toasted Millet

Sara Strother, yogaview instructor

Among the fruits and vegetables richest in health-promoting antioxidants, cranberries rank at the top of the list. This wheat- and dairy-free cornbread gives you another easy way to bring more cranberries into your diet. —Sara

Preparation time: 10 minutes
Total time: 1 hour 10 minutes

2 cups fine ground cornmeal
½ cup coarse ground cornmeal
2 cups spelt flour
¾ cup toasted millet
3 tablespoons baking powder
1 teaspoon sea salt

1¼ cup filtered water
1⅓ cup unsweetened rice milk
⅔ cup safflower oil
½ cup grade B maple syrup
1 cup fresh cranberries

Preheat oven to 400°. Lightly oil a 9 x 13-inch baking dish. Sift dry ingredients (except berries) and add wet ingredients. Mix well and fold in berries.

Bake for 50 minutes. Let sit 10 minutes before cutting.

Pumpernickel Bread

Bob Mark, friend of yogaview

It's worth it to seek out organic flours for this recipe (and for your cooking in general)—it's a simple way to avoid synthetic fertilizers, herbicides, and pesticides in your food, while supporting grain producers whose practices consider the health of our environment. And your bread will taste much better! —Bob

Preparation time: 20 minutes
Total time: 10-24 hours
Serves 8-10

3 cups white flour
½ cup rye flour
1 ¼ teaspoon salt
1 ¼ teaspoon dry active yeast
1 tablespoon powdered cocoa
1 tablespoon instant espresso
   coffee grounds

1 cup warm water
1 tablespoon dark molasses
1 cup room temperature club soda
corn meal or white flour for dusting cloth
1 or 2 tablespoons caraway seeds

Place all the dry ingredients in a large mixing bowl and mix together. Stir the molasses into the cup of warm water. Add the liquids into the dry ingredients and stir them together into a lumpy, damp ball (not soggy or overly wet). If there are dry ingredients left, gradually add more warm water until all are damp. Cover bowl with a damp cloth or plastic wrap and place in a dark, minimum 70° location for anywhere from 6-18 hours (I prefer 16-18 hours; some say more of the gluten is eaten by the dry active yeast).

Next, place the dough on a clean dish towel dusted with corn meal or flour so the dough won't stick to the cloth. Sprinkle with caraway seeds and fold in half. Sprinkle again and again, fold in half. Return to bowl (washed and dried) and sprinkle with caraway seeds. Cover with cloth or plastic wrap and return to dark, warm location for 2-4 hours.

During this time, heat a 6-quart Dutch oven or heavy metal pot with a cover or pottery casserole with cover to 500° for 30-45 minutes. Pull out the rack, remove the cover, and flip the dough into it (it may look ragged but the heat will even it out). Cover and put in oven for 30-40 minutes or until it gets darker and "thumps" when tapped with your finger. Now remove the cover and return to oven for 10-20 minutes until the interior is dry when tested with a long toothpick. Remove from the oven and let rest with cover off. Cut, butter, and enjoy!

Candied Chipotle Walnuts

Vivian Roumboulas, yogaview student

Walnuts are a great way to get more unsaturated fats, omega-3 fatty aids, fiber, and vitamin E into your diet. —Vivian

Preparation time: 5 minutes
Total time: 1 hour, 20 minutes
Makes 3-4 cups

1 lb. organic walnut halves
1 cup dark brown sugar
½ cup granulated sugar
1 teaspoon chipotle chili powder

1 ¼ teaspoon kosher salt
1 teaspoon water
1 egg white

Preheat oven to 350°. Whisk egg white with 1 teaspoon water until frothy (not stiff). Combine sugars, salt, and chili powder in a bowl until blended well. Toss walnuts with egg white mixture, then sugar mixture.

Lay out evenly on sheet pan lined with parchment. Bake for about 30-40 minutes, until fragrant and dark brown but not burnt.

Allow to cool for 30 minutes, then break apart and store in airtight container.

Refreshing Watermelon Juice

Dorie Silverman, yogaview instructor

Watermelon is 92 percent water and is high in the super antioxidant lycopene– this simple juice beats sports drinks for health and hydration any day! —Dorie

Preparation time: 5 minutes
Total time: 5 minutes
Serves 2

2 cups cubed watermelon, chilled
6-8 mint leaves

Blend mint and watermelon in a blender. Enjoy!

Acknowledgments

Jenny Boeder, Vivian Roumboulas, Michael Flockhart, Claire Mark

When I first decided to put together a cookbook, I had no idea how much work and time would actually be required to make it happen. When I told my long-time friend and fellow yogaview teacher Jenny Boeder about the book, she immediately offered to edit it. That was the best gift I could have asked for. In the last year I have thought a million times over that if it weren't for Jenny, this book never would have been made. She became not only editor and writer but project manager, overseeing every aspect of this process from beginning to end. Her endless support, hard work, and constant excitement about the book made this dream a reality.

We were so fortunate to have Vivian Roumboulas on the team as our recipe tester, food consultant, and chef extraordinaire—her discerning palate, recipe fine-tuning, original culinary creations, and exacting standards took this book to a whole new level of excellence. I'm grateful to Michael Flockhart, friend and fellow yogaview instructor, for his superb design skills—I gained a whole new appreciation for his creativity and artistic nature. And it wouldn't be a yogaview project without Scott Shigley, my favorite photographer! Scott is not only a brilliant artist, but his flexibility and humor made the photo shoots a total pleasure.

I am enormously indebted to all the teachers, friends, chefs, restaurateurs, and family members who donated their recipes to this book—without all of you, this book wouldn't exist, and I thank you from the bottom of my heart. Special thanks in particular to pastry chef and yogaview student Erik Hecimovich for donating so many of his wonderful and original dessert recipes!

I am so grateful for the love and support of my sister, Tara Mark. She was 100% encouraging about my book idea, and her enthusiasm kept me energized about the project even when I felt overwhelmed. Huge thanks also to my parents for raising me in a home where healthy, good food was a priority and family dinners a must, and to my dear friend Dana Weiner, who donated her beautiful pottery for us to use in the photos.

Finally, heartfelt thanks goes to my partner, Quinn Kearney. When we first moved in together I was not a great cook. His constant appreciation of the food I made and his encouragement to keep cooking is what made me so excited to keep getting back in the kitchen!

Cooking Up Change

10% of the proceeds from *Cooking with a yogaview* go to support **Cooking Up Change.** Cooking Up Change began as a Chicago cooking contest but has expanded to cities across the country. Created by the Healthy Schools Campaign, the contest challenges public school students to create a great-tasting lunch that meets nutrition standards on a tight budget, using only ingredients commonly available for school food service (think "Top Chef" for teenagers). Students must create recipes that include no more than six steps so that they can easily be replicated on a large scale in real school kitchens. (Go to page 19 to see "Soup of Sunshine," an award-winning recipe created by Cooking Up Change student chefs!)

We chose Cooking Up Change as our beneficiary because we are huge supporters of their mission: educating young people about food and health; bringing nutritious, real food to public school students; and fighting to reform our national school food policy. We strongly encourage all of you who care about getting healthier food to American kids to go to *healthyschoolscampaign.org*, where you can volunteer, donate, and get tickets to the Cooking Up Change gala, and sample the delicious culinary creations of these remarkable student chefs! (As for non-Chicagoans: Cooking Up Change has now spread to many cities across the country, so check their website to see how you might get involved in your area.)

healthyschoolscampaign.org

Other resources:

yogaview.com
greengrocerchicago.com
familyfarmed.org
thepublicanrestaurant.com
lulacafe.com
avecrestaurant.com
townshipchicago.com
shigleyphoto.com
flockhartdesign.com
cookingwithayogaview.com

Index of Vegan Recipes

57 total

All of the recipes below are either vegan or can be prepared vegan with a simple substitution. We've noted these substitutions in the recipe directions (i.e.,"to make vegan, substitute avocado for cheese") but still suggest reading through all ingredients carefully to be sure they are in line with your dietary needs.

Index of Gluten-Free Recipes
74 total

All of the recipes below are either gluten-free or can be prepared gluten-free with a simple omission or substitution (i.e., using gluten-free buns or omitting them entirely from Portobello Mushroom Burgers). If you have a serious gluten allergy, you should read through all ingredients carefully and consult your physician to confirm they fit your dietary needs.